Jenson Speed

FIVE MOVES FOR LUCY

FIVE MOVES FOR LUCY

Front Cover drawings by Adrian Timbers

A story about a married couple Jenson and Hollie Speed, highlighting, the many problems they had to encounter in their 13 year quest to adopt a child. Names of all persons living or dead in this story has been changed to protect individuals anonymity.

FIVE MOVES FOR LUCY

CONTENTS

FIVE MOVES FOR LUCY

The Start Of Our Journey

Looking back one cannot help but smile, when we, Hollie and Jenson Speed started out, just like everybody else I suppose. we had absolutely no idea how things were going to work out in our lives. we met fell in love got married, just a small affair with just a handful of friends and family present, we didn't have a huge amount of money in those early days, even if we had plenty of money, a flashy wedding would not have been a top priority for us, the most valuable thing to us was, we were in love, that was the most important thing.

We now both feel that our marriage despite our ups and downs has been the really best thing that we could possibly have asked for in our lives, however, life was hard for us throughout the 1960's and 1970's, even so, there was one definite blessing, there were any amount of jobs, one could pick and choose, people could quite easily leave a job in the morning and have another one by the afternoon, how different from today when many young people are having enormous problems finding a job.

We started out working in the hotel and restaurant industry this enabled us to see various parts of the country without having to buy or rent a house as we only picked jobs where staff could live in, sometimes we lived in hotel rooms, in other hotels and restaurants they had staff accommodation such as a flat or a staff cottage or even a caravan in the grounds.

One big drawback however, was that the hours were usually excessively long and generally incredibly poorly paid, we often started work in the early morning at six o'clock preparing breakfasts mainly for business representatives who usually made a particularly early start, going all around the country to sell their wares, after breakfast, we would clear all that away, then prepare for morning coffee, followed by lunch, this was normally a very busy time as business people would bring their potential customers to the hotel or restaurant and lush them up with lots of food and wine, in those days, sometimes they would have an enormous amount of people present, the wine would flow very often all afternoon and on into the late evening, so a lunch would flow right on until their evening meal.
I understand that it was very favourable at that time because all of this wining and dining could be claimed against tax as a business expense,

I think nowadays that it only applies when treating foreign guests. Lunch for those who were not at these business meals was followed by afternoon teas, these once again were always busy, as in those days lots of people, especially the elderly folk would meet up with their friends for afternoon tea, not just tea they would also have a large selection of cakes on up too four tier cake stands, others would have scones with usually strawberry jam with a large dollop of fresh clotted cream.

After serving teas we would normally have had a break of about two hours then back to work to prepare for dinner to be served in the evenings, with us both then working often late into the night, many nights not finishing till around ten thirty or eleven o'clock, some nights we would leave off work being really shattered.

On occasions we would also be required too work extra hours at weekends to help with weddings and functions. You might have heard the saying 'The good old days' it certainly was for many people, but for those who had to look after these people, it was extremely hard work.

Looking back despite it being like a slave camp with remarkably little time off, nevertheless we both enjoyed it immensely, as the people we met were so varied from millionaires, bosses of huge businesses, pop stars, families having a special special treat, solicitors, members of parliament, doctors, surgeons and vicars. We also met a huge amount of people, at birthday parties and weddings, it was good training for us meeting and talking to a whole wealth of individuals from a dustman to a duke a lollypop lady to a princess, we both were able to learn an awful lot regarding how to deal with and talk to people from every walk of life. We carried on in the hotel and restaurant trade for a few years before settling down in a rented old style cottage situated in the country on the edge of a city. I then started an ice cream business with just one van.

I absolutely loved it, Hollie used to help me as time allowed, as she also had a part time job and looked after our home and of course she cooked all of our meals. The best bit about the ice cream business was meeting all of the youngsters, I had a regular round, 'Ding Dong, Ding Dong' same place, same time, around housing estates from around eleven in the morning, except for a couple of small breaks, right through too around nine o'clock at night, I worked five days on the round each week, having just one day off, then on a Sunday, usually my busiest day, I would park up all day at a riverside beauty spot where I would have scores of people in a queue for most of the day on sunny days, if it rained or if it was cold, I would revert back to my regular round. In those days I sold ice cream for twelve months of the year, even going out in the deep winter snow and ice.

A must was that I always took a snow shovel with me in case I got stuck in the snow, the mainstay in the winter was selling blocks of ice cream, as most people in those days didn't have a home freezer, therefore, with me coming along their street or road at the same time of day on a regular basis this enabled customers to buy these ice cream blocks as a treat for the families tea, they would cut them up so that each family member could have a slice each, often along with some tinned peaches, apricots or pineapple. The ice cream blocks came in a variety of different flavours, vanilla, strawberry, blackcurrant, chocolate and a real favourite, neopolitan, a striped multi-flavour and colour block of ice cream.

During my work, going round the housing estates, I met hundreds if not thousands of mums and dads and their children, scores would wait for me despite more posh flashy ice cream vans going round in front of me, there was something rather nice about that, perhaps it was the multi-coloured hundreds and thousands that I dipped the little children's ice cream in, I also sold ice lollypops, crisps, sweets, chocolate, candy floss and toffee apples.

It ended up that after a period of around four years having during that time I purchased a total of five ice cream vans and I leased a former milk depot with huge fridges and freezers, which I used as my business headquarters, however, once I started to employ staff, after extensive checks, I found out that some of the staff had started to dip into the tills, I had very little control over this as cash was involved, I reluctantly decided to sell the business.

Selling the business enabled us to open up one of the very first whole-food restaurants in our nearest city centre, followed by taking over the catering side of an extremely popular public house, bang in the centre of the city next to all of the major department stores.

Our marriage was exceptionally good, we got on very well as a couple, nevertheless, there was one huge problem Hollie had a number of miscarriages, we went through all of the necessary medical checks, advice and treatment resulting in us finally having a little boy, we named him Stephen, quite sadly after only three days Stephen died.

This was followed by an unsettling time for Hollie, the restaurants became too much for us both, that is why they had to go, nevertheless, our lives had to go on, it was around this time that we discussed together the possibility of adopting a child, but nothing became of it, I suppose the time was not right. I got a job working for a local authority in their housing department, I didn't like the job one little bit, in fact it frustrated me, at the enormous amount of money that I had to waste on their behalf, over the years, many millions of pounds.

Hollie in the meantime worked in several different jobs, but she never really settled in any of them, we always did put a little cash away for rainy days, as most people did in those days, after a few years we managed to save enough money to put down as a deposit on a bungalow which was on the edge of a pretty little town. It was rather like in many recent years mortgages were hard to get, we were turned down by many banks and building societies, however, we stuck to our guns and eventually found a small building society based in London who were prepared to help us with a mortgage, this enabled us to purchase the very first home that we could call our own. We also got our very first pet dog a bit like a sheepdog, we named her Cindy.

It was at this time that I started to take a real interest in gardening, enabling me to grow lots of tasty organic vegetables, to this day that has never left me, I love working in the garden.

We Were having The Good Life

My dear late father was a particularly keen farmer and gardener as was my grandfather before him, I suppose that is where my love of gardening comes from, Hollie used to look after the flower garden and pot plants and I concentrated on the growing of vegetables we shared the task of cutting the lawn. We both worked hard on making the bungalow a much nicer, brighter and more comfortable place to live by knocking two small reception rooms into one nice size lounge, we also had fitted full central heating.

I continued to work for the local authority. however, after a few years we decided to move, Cindy sadly died of old age, I buried her in our lovely garden and planted an apple tree on top of her, because of not wanting her ever to be disturbed, she was faithful to her last breath. Bless her.

We then moved from our bungalow into a beautiful country cottage in an incredibly pretty valley situated in the middle of stunning countryside, it was delightful and it had a large garden with tip top rich black soil, ideal for growing organic vegetables, which I planted, We then fitted a wood burning Rayburn cooker, which became Hollie's pride and joy, she would make lots of superb meals using my home grown delicious vegetables, we were having the good life.

Unfortunately all was not well, problems soon began to arise, opposite to the cottage was a large arable farm, we were obviously very aware of this when we purchased the cottage, however, we were not aware that he was expanding his business fast. He put up up half a dozen huge grain dryers and a massive potato store, just like an aircraft hangar only a few metres away from our gorgeous cottage.

At harvest time he would constantly pump grain from one dryer too another, the grain made an awful racket as it was pumped along the metal tubes between these huge grain dryers, at night we could never open our bedroom windows because of the tremendous constant clattering noise from these grain dryers, it would keep us both awake.

Sadly Our Dream Cottage Turned Out To Be A Living Nightmare

Then came the potato harvest, this massive potato store that the farmer had built, had louvre doors at either end, with the potato storage area of the building being underground in the centre of this building, the edifice had a huge wind turbine built horizontally within the store, when switched on and being operated, the fresh outside air would be sucked through the giant pair of louvre doors at one end of the building by this enormous wind turbine which then changed the wind direction on downwards and on through the underground stored potato's which were stored in huge wooden crates and then on up again, then finally the air was blown out through the other pair of louvre doors at the other end of the building.

It was like a jumbo jet taking off 24/7, in addition the farmer would constantly spray our cottage with huge jets of water as he watered his potatoe's with one of those massive hose gadgets that move automatically from one end of a field to the other, it would splash against our windows and cause flooding near our front door, that used to make Hollie hopping mad as it would leave the windows when they dried out with all streaky water stains on them and if we accidentally ever forgot to close the windows water would splash inside the cottage.
Worse still this farmer had a mobile contraption like a moon buggy which had large extended arms on either side of it, he would sit inside this machine looking like an astronaut having on his special suit and helmet, the spray from this thing would blow all over my organic vegetable plot.

I would constantly call at the farmers door to complain about these things, he would just shrug his shoulders and in a sort of unhelpful manner while telling me "That is farming for you, if people want food to eat, they will have to put up with these things"I was in fact the last person in the world who would have bought his awful chemical laced potatoe's.
I found him to be irksome and unbelievably hard to deal with, he even said to me, " I was here before you," Sadly our dream cottage turned out to be a living nightmare, we were not happy at all living there, even so, at the time we were not in any sort of financial position to move house.
One day Hollie came up to me and said "Jenson, what can I do? I would

like to work from home, I do not want to go to work anymore," I had known instinctively for some time that she was not happy with the work she was doing, despite her not complaining about it. Hollie is a gem, she just gets on with things, nevertheless, it was now very obvious to me from her speaking out in this way that she wanted a total change.

I had in fact been thinking and turning over in my mind for several months business ideas that might suit Hollie, something that she could do from home, I said to her "Why don't you let out holiday cottages on behalf of other people, start up a holiday cottage letting agency."
Little did I know that what I had just said would be an enormous turning point in our lives, it would change our lives forever. From the small front bedroom of our little country cottage a holiday letting agency was about to be born.
We spent several days just discussing what we had to do to get this off the ground, we had precious little cash, but buckets full of enthusiasm, we had to buy a typewriter, I managed to buy one from a secondhand shop, paper and envelopes and that was about it, we then set about typing out then neatly folding agreements for the owners of the holiday homes to agree to and sign.
We then placed a three line classified advertisement in our local newspaper. 'Wanted Holiday Cottages' from a couple of these tiny advertisements we managed to get a total of ten cottages, we put these in a homemade brochure with pictures of these ten cottages hand drawn by myself with details of the cottages printed out on our trusty secondhand typewriter. Next we put a little matchbox size advertisement in a major national Sunday newspaper, 'Holiday Cottages To Let' the telephone calls came in thick and fast, shortly afterwards followed by our very first booking, Bingo! That was enough for Hollie to hand in her notice at work. The rest is history Hollies business went from strength to strength.

I helped Hollie with every spare hour that I could muster, I used to go out and meet cottage owners normally at weekends or when I had days off from work or when I was on holiday from work, sometimes I would even call on cottage owners during the light evenings in the event that they were out at work during the day.
It took us around five years to get the business up to a grand total of three hundred and fifty cottages on our book, at this point I handed in my notice at work and joined Hollie full time in the business.

We had already by this time sold the cottage and purchased an office with an adjacent house on the outskirts of a small town, this proved to be an exceedingly wise move, because there was absolutely no way that we could

6

have taken on staff and managed to cope with the running of the business from the bedroom of our small country cottage, in any case were awfully glad to move away from that troublesome farm.

The equipment that we were then using was state of the art computers, copiers, fax machines, full colour glossy brochures were printed, all a far cry from when we first started the business. We had also at this stage taken on a number of friendly staff they became the absolute lifeblood of the business, they never watched the clock, absolute gems, lovely honest people, we will never forget them as long as we live.

Our Life Was About To Change Once Again This Time Quite Dramatically

They worked all hours, in fact they worked their socks off for the enhancement of the business, often working late into the night to make sure that everything was kept up to date. We still keep in touch with them, going to our youngest member of staffs wedding, she in fact started working for us on leaving school and remained faithful to us all of the time that we were running the business.

In fact Hollie and myself ran the holiday home agency for a total of eleven years, then because the business had outgrown us and we were working exceptionally long hours often late into the night, we were both really tired, we decided to sell the business. During those working years we also managed to buy a delightful house in the country, life was very enjoyable, we also during those years attained another beautiful pet dog a Golden Labrador she was adorable we named her Sally.

However our life was about to change once again this time quite dramatically. The business was remarkably easy to sell, in fact we had several potential buyers, most were already in the holiday business and wanted to purchase our business and move our agency from its existing base in order to combine it with their holiday business.

That would mean that our faithful members of staff would have been out of a job, we said No! to many potential buyers, stating, 'If you want the business you will have too buy the business and premises, lock, stock and barrel and run it from the same premises and carry on employing the existing staff.'

Many refused, nevertheless, we need not have worried as a particularly nice guy from London, bought the business, he then promoted all of the existing staff to run the business, He asked me if I could oversee the business for the first three months of him taking over. I gladly said "Yes," he would telephone me around once a week, just to check on progress, in fact he barely set a foot in the place, he had complete confidence in the staff, he ran it this way for a further ten years and eventually sold it on to another local holiday agency and some of our former staff worked for yet again new owners, so all is well that ends well.

Our attention now turned once again to the thought of adopting a child, we thought that we would now have the time and the energy too devote to a little boy or girl or both now that we had sold the business.

The year was 1990 we decided to move from East Anglia to Scotland, Scotland, I hear you ask? Why? Well let me explain.

Many years ago we had a truly remarkable good friend named Tom, he was a lovely, lovely man, in fact he was a real gentleman, we had never before, nor since had such a loyal friend, he used to visit our home most days, in fact he was just like a brother, anyhow,Tom got married to a Welsh girl and we lost complete track of him.

Several years later on an elderly friend of Hollie named Betty, asked me if I could possibly drive her to Wales, a trip of some two hundred and fifty miles from East Anglia for her to visit a friend of hers, I instantly agreed as I also wanted to visit some other friends of ours, Doreen and John, who had a number of years ago moved to Wales and bought a house there and they lived just a couple of miles away from Betty's friend.

I would not only be helping this dear lady Betty, it would give me the chance to visit these dear old friends of mine who I hadn't seen for several years. I could kill two birds with one stone.

Hollie didn't come with us, on arriving at our destination in Wales, I dropped Betty off at her friends house and then I proceeded to visit Doreen and her husband John at their home, on arrival the first thing that they said to me was, "Did I know that Tom was acutely ill in a hospital in Scotland with only three days to live," I didn't even take my coat off, I apologised, then said my goodbyes, I then rushed back to see Betty and informed her of the situation that I was off to Scotland and I would pick her up later.

I drove the car up to Scotland as quickly as I could, I had in fact never ever been to Scotland before in my life so it was all new to me, on arriving at the hospital I found our dear, dear friend seriously ill, Tom had a plastic mask over his mouth and nose, through which he was desperately gasping for breath. I was told by the doctor that he had the lung condition asbestosis Pneumoconiosis caused by the inhalation of asbestos dust, to help to alleviate his symptoms they were giving him oxygen and water in a sort of mist through this mask on his face, in fact his poor face was red raw all around the area where the mast touched his skin. He recognised me and tried hard to give me a little smile. I felt really helpless, here was this kind, gentle man critically ill, I do remember Tom telling me that he had a job

8

when he was younger making sheds and chicken huts using timber and asbestos sheets, I suppose back then nobody realised the immense danger that this stuff posed, when it was sawn or drilled, poor Tom was now paying the price, little did he know that the work that he was doing at that time would eventually kill him.

I met his wife Linda there, in fact I soon realised that I had known her from years previous, she invited me to stay at their home, a grand old stone built farmhouse situated in the country, I was very grateful because it was getting late and I had made no prior plans on where I was going to stay. I phoned Hollie and said "I am in Scotland" "You are where!" she said, bearing in mind she thought that I was in Wales.

It Was To Be Tom's Very Last Visit To See His Favourite Seaside Places

I then explained to her all about our dear friend Tom, that he was in hospital with probably only a short while to live, she was really upset by this very sad news. Tom lived for a further three months, I was able to visit him by getting on an aircraft at Norwich airport and fly up to Scotland, then hire a car and get Bed and Breakfast accommodation near to the hospital, I found this to be a particularly convenient way to visit my dear friend Tom, I visited him on three separate occasions, however after the latest trip to see Tom, I didn't know, but this was going to be the very last visit to see him, the hospital had sent him home because they said that they could no longer do anything for him.

On this last visit, Tom asked me, despite having great difficulty speaking, if I could take him to his favourite seaside villages on the coast, I said without a moments hesitation "I would love to" it took me about a half an hour to get dear Tom out of the house and into the car, he was a seriously sick man gasping for breath, even so, with sheer effort and determination on his part, he made it.

I then took Tom to the seaside, it was not very far when using the car, Tom absolutely loved every moment of this little trip out, despite his suffering, he said very few words, but he smiled quite a lot, however it was to be Toms very last visit to see his favourite seaside places. I must say, I was also absolutely enthralled by the sheer rugged, breathtaking, awe inspiring beauty of these delightful villages, I had no idea at the time that being here with Tom that day in some tiny seaside villages in Scotland would eventually change my life forever.

Our dear friend Tom passed away shortly afterwards, I remember sadly thinking, why do the good die so young? he was fifty eight, that is no great age nowadays, nevertheless, he did say to me before he died, that he had never been so happy in all of his life, than the time he spent walking with his faithful old dog along that breathtaking coastline. I was eternally grateful that I was able to take some photographs of Tom with his loyal pet dog during the last few days of his life and to spend those very special treasured moments with him. Some years previously Tom had given me a little framed print print of a male and female linnet sitting on a gorse bush by an artist named Tom Banks, I regularly take that down from my office wall, ponder on it for a while and just contemplate and reflect on the real pleasure I got from just knowing that I was a very fortunate man indeed and deeply glad in my heart to have been a good friend of this humble, lovely, remarkably, special gentleman. Hollie felt exactly the same way about our dear friend Tom, he will be treasured in both of our hearts always.

At a later date we purchased some pretty holiday cottages in one of Toms favourite villages, I rented them out to holiday makers, so that other people could also enjoy the sheer wonder of this little known area.

Hollie and myself used to visit the cottages every April and again in the November, when we had the holiday agency, it gave us an early and a late season break, we had some really great memorable holidays on this stretch of glorious coastline, the sea most days seemed to be a lovely green and blue colour and dolphins could be seen most days.

Sunrises were a sight for sore eyes, in fact a joy to behold as the sun seemed to gently rise up from the sea, this fantastic huge red ball of fire, made the sea light up looking like it was on fire, what an extraordinary, stunning, spectacle.

I remember very well one day searching and finding eighteen different kinds of seaweed growing amongst the coastal rocks near to the beach and sea, much of it was rich in the most spectacular different colours, from the deepest greens, bright reds even the brown ones had a fantastic sheen that flashed brightly in the sunlight.

I also found masses of small fish, shells of every description hiding amongst the rocks, there was also an abundance of starfish and scores of other little creatures, I was in my element.

A local lady looked after the cottages for us, she lovingly cleaned them and cared for them between lets, sorted out any problems and looked after the people when on their holiday. We had visitors books, peoples comments were always upbeat, many returned year on year.

So, that is the reason why after we sold our holiday agency we decided to move to Scotland and then proceed with our proposed plans, our great desire to adopt a child. We then purchased a grand old house on the outskirts of a small town. Little did we know that we were both about to embark on one of the biggest battles of our lives.

We Always Thought In Our Minds That To Adopt A Child Would Be An Easy Thing To Do

We had always wanted children of our own, but it was not possible, we had discussed together many times that maybe adoption was the best way forward, we discounted immediately the thought of fostering a child, mainly because Hollie would have hated the thought of just getting to know a little boy or girl, grow fond of them, knowing Hollie she would get to love them, only then to have them taken away, it would have broken her heart.

We always thought in our minds that to adopt a child would be an easy thing to do? We decided that when we get settled in our new home in Scotland, we would get the ball rolling and try to adopt a child, we considered that this would be the icing on the cake of our lives.

The move to Scotland had its problems our pet golden Labrador Sally was extremely ill on the very morning that we were moving house, in fact the huge removal lorry was almost fully loaded, when our dear Sally just suddenly with no warning toppled over, Hollie also said to me that she didn't feel very well, I thought that it was probably the stress of moving house. I said to Hollie "I am sorry love, I know that you are not feeling very well but I am going to have to take Sally to the vets" our vet was about five miles away. I had no idea at this point that Hollie was really quite ill.

I arrived at the vets and carried our Sally in to his surgery, the vet was unbelievably kind and helpful, I was able to see him immediately, he examined Sally, he then said, with a solemn expression on his face, "I am really sorry, but she is going to die," I could hardly believe my ears, he then said, "It would be kinder to put her to sleep right now" I had no choice our beautiful Sally just fell over yet again, the vet put our Sally to sleep.

I was absolutely devastated, it was such an unexpected shock, with tears running down my cheeks, I carried Sally's lifeless body in a green plastic sack back to the car. I wanted Hollie to see her just one last time and then to bury her in her favourite spot in the garden.

On arriving back at the house Hollie looked extremely pale and was being sick, I didn't want to tell her that our Sally had too be put to sleep, because she already had enough on her plate with her sickness, regretfully, I felt that I had to tell her, I had absolutely no option, she would have

11

asked where Sally was, I broke the news to her as gently as I possibly could, she took it quite badly, enough for me too immediately telephone a friend, who came straight away and looked after her, the removal men were still a work filling the removal lorry.

I then had the unenviable job of digging a big hole in the garden, remembering Sallys favourite spot, never did I think that the ground was so unforgiving, it was like rock, there were tree roots, stones, every spade full of soil removed was a huge effort, but I was determined that was where our Sally would be buried, I didn't need a spade I needed a pickaxe.

Sally Will Never Set Foot In Our New House In Scotland

I was crying I just couldn't hold back the tears, thinking that our dear Sally will never set foot in our new home in Scotland, Hollie despite being poorly insisted that she gave her Sally a final hug and a kiss, followed by a big hug and kiss from me. Goodbye our best friend, it was very sad.

I planted some flowers on the top of Sallys grave, making it look the same as the surrounding garden, what a wonderful, Wonderful friend. Rest In Peace.

I then helped the removal men by firstly making them some more tea and biscuits, I then helped them with a large heavy wardrobe, the only things then remaining to load, were garden items, wheel barrow, garden tools, ride on mower and several garden pots full of flowers, plants and cuttings I always liked when moving house, to take some sentimental plants that used to belong to mum and dad, grandmother and grandfather.

I suppose that deep down I am a sentimental old thing, but I must say that I cannot think of anything nicer than to have reminders of people you loved, right before your very eyes every time you venture out into your garden, for people with no garden, the same can be done with the use of garden pots. I know after dad died, mum couldn't look after his very large garden, so she had it put down to grass, then she had instead a vast area of pot plants, the pots were of all different heights, so she had the large ones at the back right down to the smaller ones at the front, they looked a picture and some of those same plants are on their way to Scotland

I then done a final search of the house to make sure that nothing had been missed, finally I had the job of giving the house a thorough good clean out, Hollie normally done a final clean, however, on this occasion I had to do it, because while I was doing this our helpful friend had taken Hollie to the local doctors surgery, the verdict, she must go home and go to bed and rest, Hollie said to the doctor,"I cannot do that, I have to move to Scotland over six hundred miles away, we have to be out of our house by twelve o'clock.

Move Number One

The removal lorry left on its two day trip to Scotland, and a short while later, after saying our goodbyes to friends, we locked our front door for the very last time and armed with a couple of camp beds and some blankets and all the things needed to make a cup of tea, we set off.

We had a six hundred and fifty mile journey ahead of us, I asked Hollie if she would rather go in a hotel for a day, she declined and wanted to get going. It was a really horrendous journey.

Hollie was sick every few miles, I had to keep stopping in parking places and service stations, with all the stopping it took us over twelve hours to reach our new home, once again I asked Hollie if she wanted to stay in a hotel for the rest of the night, "No,"she insisted, she wanted to go to her new home.

On arriving at our new home, I quickly erected camp beds, helped Hollie into bed, I then wrapped extra blankets around her and put a pillow under her head, she was looking extremely poorly.

I immediately then proceeded to find a doctor, thankfully he came to the house fairly quickly, he gave Hollie an injection, she soon went off into a deep sleep, she had a good night, thankfully.

I got up the next morning and started to give the house a bit of a clean, I couldn't do a lot only pick up by hand any bits laying around as all of our cleaning tools and stuff was still on the road, then I went and done a little shopping, I had no meals to cook for Hollie as she was not eating anything, I then went out and had a bite to eat myself, later in the day the removal lorry arrived, looking after Hollie was my first priority, the doctor called in again and gave her another injection she was still looking in a poor way.

The removal men soon started unloading the boxes which were all numbered from the removal lorry, I did try and explain to the men where I wanted everything, however Hollie would have normally organized where each and every box would go, but because of the circumstances, it was my job, boxes were coming into the house like they were on a factory conveyor belt, dozens of boxes were being piled ever higher in all the wrong places, it was like organized chaos.

I then helped the removal men to put up our big double bed so that Hollie could get a good nights sleep, and it seemed as if, I was never going to stop making tea with huge amounts of sugar and dishing out chocolate coated digestive biscuits, the removal men certainly like their sweet tea and biscuits. After what seemed like an eternity the last items finally came off the removal lorry, I thanked the men gave them a tip and off they went back to England.

It took around three weeks and several more visits from the doctor for

Hollie to fully recover, we never discovered what caused her illness.
We absolutely loved the house, it took a while to sort it out, unpacking
the huge amount of boxes seemed to take forever, but we won in the end
and our great adventure was about to begin.
We spent several weeks getting the house pretty well straight we then
contacted social services, a few more weeks past they then got in touch
with us, saying that a social worker would call.

The day finally arrived a social worker named Christine Strange called,
we said our hello's and shortly after that she informed us that she thought
that we were probably too old to adopt a child, I was forty seven and
Hollie was forty four, in our wildest dreams we never thought that our
ages would be an obstacle that could stop us from adopting a child,
I was thinking, many pop stars, father children well into their seventies,
Nevertheless we persisted telling her that we would at least like to try
to be considered to adopt a child, resulting in the two of us attending
assessment meetings with endless questions over and over again for
about eighteen months.

With this social worker we had to go through a questionnaire format
that was created by an agency for adoption and fostering this assessment
document is a home study that can be difficult, exacting, burdensome
and intrusive, notwithstanding, in the hands of a caring social worker
or perhaps someone with a bit more experience in dealing with people,
it could be almost a pleasure to go through, however, in the hands of a
social worker who probably thought that we were too old at the onset, it
was at times a little unpleasant, could this have possibly been because her
training could have been of a better quality and understanding we got the
distinct impression that she might have thought that it was all a waste of
her time?
Hollie and myself were determined to try and adopt a child, so we went
through the various questions answering to the best of our ability with
honest answers, however, with hindsight, I think that both Hollie and
myself would have always been truthful, as we both believe that telling
the truth is extremely important, even so, there were times when we
would have definitely held back just a little bit or perhaps being a trifle
more selective regarding the answers we gave to the questions posed, the
reason being, everything that we said was analysed by this social worker,
in huge depth, it was scrutinized, torn apart, probed, examined,
investigated, dissected and broken down into minute tiny parts, then each
of these tiny part was further torn apart this was then gone over repeatedly
often for many weeks.

For instance we both found the repeat questioning about our deceased son Stephen quite upsetting, in fact nauseating, the social worker went over and over and over the subject of our son Stephens death for endless weeks, Where did he die? How did he die? Where is he buried, the questions just kept on coming, Why aren't you crying? We informed her that we had done our crying and had our moments of sadness many years previously, time helps to heal these unforeseen circumstances.

We were both made to feel that we did not love and care about our little boy a comforting scripture for us is; John Chapter 5 verses 28 & 29.
One has to get over these unhappy times, because time and unforeseen circumstances can indeed happen to anybody, I perhaps do not expect that there are many social workers who can fully understand what we and other people believe, whatever that belief is, because of their overpowering attitude, using instead, vague probing questions and never really fully understanding what individuals really sincerely believe.
It has got to be better for all people, whoever we are, who come through difficult periods in our lives, to try hard by not dwelling on those now past sad and troubled times, one can probably never ever forget what has happened, just the same we all have a future, therefore isn't it vitally important that we all strive hard to have a fulfilling happy future rather than being sad all of the time. There are indeed better times ahead, although at the moment it somehow doesn't seem like that. So why don't we all try hard to look and work towards a brighter future, we never know what is just around the next bend, there could well be a delightful answer to all of our troubles leading to everything our hearts desire.

Love Doesn't Work With These Children

That was one of the extremely important reasons why we were trying hard to adopt a child, in order to give a child who is now in care, a good future and all of our love, a future that due to circumstances totally outside of our control we could not give to our son Stephen.
The social worker also highlighted, that if a child lives on a council estate, that is where they like them to stay, meaning that a child who lived on such an estate, would probably never be able to come and live with us, because we did not live on a council estate, at the time we were shocked at such revelations.
As we got a deeper knowledge of how the adoption system operated, Nothing shocked us, we now realise, that one could have the wrong colour skin, the child could have the wrong colour skin, wrong culture, one might be white middle class, live in the wrong kind of house, wrong faith, over

weight and so on, shocking is not a strong enough word, all of the children in care need at least a chance and a level playing field to be part of a loving forever family. The assessment continued.

These assessments cover subjects like, have you any experience in looking after children, how could one give a child a safe and caring environment, religion, adoption is forever, previous relationships, health, wealth, working as part of a team, family, brothers sister, parents, childhood, what kind of child do you want? That is just a very small taste of the questions posed.

Amongst these many hundreds of questions the social worker put to us, one was, how would we go about helping a newly adopted child?

Our reply was, 'To show the child or children as much love as possible, she answered saying "Love doesn't work with these children," we were both shocked by such a thought she was talking as if every one of the children in care push away emotions. Therefore she thought, and indeed told us that we were both very naïve to think that love shown towards an adopted child was the answer, in fact she highlighted this specific point about our naivety regarding showing love towards these children when writing about us in her report.

Well as naive means, with natural or unaffected simplicity especially in thought manners and speech, guileless, immature, inexperienced, born yesterday, childlike, wet behind the ears and gullible, admittedly we, Hollie and I, might have been a trifle inexperienced with children at that time, in fact no different from any couple who have their own first child, they also have zero experience, but hopefully they go on to show love towards their new baby.

I hasten to add that we always spoke to children and in our previous work had dealings with many thousands of children.

Love Never Fails

My sister adopted two boys with whom Hollie and myself always had an excellent loving relationship, and now they are both young men, we still have a very close relationship with them, just because they were adopted by my sister, certainly doesn't mean that they are not going to respond to being shown love, this whole way of thinking is preposterous, in fact it is an insult to both of my sisters sons who were very capable of receiving any love shown to them and also just as important they show heartfelt love to many who they come in contact with. We know for a fact that both these boys go out of their way to help those of the older generation doing things for them, for zero charge, they are both decent loving human beings. Therefore we can both say from our personal experiences in life, proven without one shadow of doubt over time, with all of the children that we have ever had dealings with, that showing them love really works, true love removes just about every obstacle in life, we have found that whatever one is doing in life, love never fails.

We have personally yet to meet a person who does not respond in some kind of positive way to being shown real heartfelt love, even so, we were very aware that some children suffer from various disorders and other complex conditions, therefore it is important to get the right answers from specialists in this field to give expert help and treatment to the child. Even so, it is essential that even if these children for some reason do not seem to accept the love from you that is shown towards them, it would be absolutely vital for one to continue to show that child as much love as humanly possible, just because a child does not accept our love, it would not mean that we would withdraw our love from them, that would be nonsensical, in fact, if we were to love someone just because they loved us of what credit would that be to us, surely, we would always need to show long suffering love in all situation, because whatever we do in life, all of our affairs should take place with love.

In fact I have been reading about a case where a couple after a number of years, having adopted a child, said that the adopted child could not form a relationship with them and that any relationship they did have with the child was they said 'Virtually non existent' note that they didn't say 'Totally non existent', therefore although very small so it seems, there was at least a teeny foundation, in order to build a good quality house a firm foundation is absolutely essential, if the house was built on sand it would undoubtedly collapse, so get the foundation right then one can proceed brick by brick.
They continued to say, when they handed the child back over to social services, commenting that the child waved goodbye, was that wave goodbye an act shown that the child had at least some kind of feeling towards the adoptive parents or an act of defiance, perhaps we will never know, however, a little spark can soon start a raging fire, love can be like that, sometimes that teeny spark has to be gently caressed, like a flint spark on some tinder dry material, by a very gentle hold and an even more gentle light blowing of air with ones mouth, it may take an awfully long time especially for the inexperienced person too succeed, but with gentle, patient, care, it can and doe's eventually burst into flame, love can be just like that.
In point of fact, one of our close friends children has downs syndrome, our

love for him, used to make his little face shine with glee every time we met him, he certainly responded to being shown our love.

In another case we experienced a long friendship with a lady who was looking after a young severely brain damaged boy who was harmed after his mother took damaging drugs while she was pregnant with him, that young lad when shown tender, loving warm affection really did respond to Hollie and myself, we used to give him cuddles and play with him, this little chap became a real loving friend.

Nobody To Love Them

Might we sincerely suggest that we were not naïve at all, this social worker Christine Strange was without a doubt the one showing naivety.

If it is the case that she and all other social workers and children's home carers as part of their training programme were being told that "Love doesn't work with these children' in care.' In our considered opinion the people who train them have sadly got it woefully wrong.

Wouldn't it be far superior if they, as part of their training had been encouraged to show much more love towards the tens of thousands of children in their care, if not, who on earth is going to show love towards these children?

Would these people who teach social workers to go out into this world to give help to these vulnerable children personally have liked it when they were children to have been brought up in a loveless world, its very hard I must admit for Hollie and me to grasp and make any sense out of this callous, hard hearted, cold hearted, unfeeling stance taken by these people towards these vulnerable children to be stuck in this awful care system with nobody to love them, it beggars belief!

In addition if social workers were to show more heartfelt respect for those people who wish to adopt these children, then perhaps a few more of these extremely vulnerable children would not have to be in foster care or remain in children's care homes, where they are often left to languish for many years, in fact many may never leave the horrible system that has been created. Children's chances of being adopted unfortunately greatly decreases as they get older.

In our case the social worker used this questionnaire form a bit like a sledge hammer, we were becoming acutely aware that prospective adoptive parents like ourselves were being put off by these extremely intrusive probes and often irrelevant checks and questions that we had too endure. If the social worker had shown a little more warmth, understanding, sensitivity and encouragement towards people like us, whose desire was to adopt a child, then perhaps she would have found loving homes for a few more of these children.

The very words social worker, surely means to be sociable, friendly, affable, sympathetic, congenial, approachable, pleasant, warm, courteous, kindly, good tempered, good humoured, gracious and mild. A social worker who strives to be good at their job, would surely want to pursue and cultivate these fine qualities, then and only then would they be in a position to help these children in care, and be the one who initially gets the ball rolling as to who is suitable to be adoptive parents, otherwise I am sad to say they are in the wrong job.

The adoption assessment meetings with this social worker went on at our home for around eighteen months, a letter then arrived from her office, stating that they had considered that it would be useful to continue on with the meetings, however, after my discussing the situation at length with Hollie we came to the conclusion that as these meetings were now covering the same ground over and over again, the meetings were becoming pointless and a complete waste of time.

All the same we discussed this with the social worker and agreed to carry on with the meetings just a little while longer, to see if if anything new would come out of these meetings.

There were in fact no new things that came up at the next few meetings, what did come up again for the umpteenth time which Hollie and myself could not agree with, as we had covered the subject at length in previous meetings, it was that we would not like a child's natural parents on the assumption that we were about to adopt a child, for those parents to be involved with that child, that went down like a lead balloon.

There were of course exceptions, for instance if a child were to lose their parents such as in an accident, those then responsible for these children might very obviously like to be involved in the child's future welfare, we discussed that we would welcome such an arrangement.

We were then told by the social worker that Scotland did not have a reciprocal arrangement with local authorities in England, in other words there was not any chance that we could adopt a child from England where there was obviously a larger amount of children available for adoption due to the much higher population fifty five million at the time.

It was suggested that we go over the points again, but we concluded that as we had already made it very clear many times that we would be prepared and extremely willing to send a child's parents a written detailed report to let them know how their son or daughter were getting on in life via a social services office anonymously.

Notwithstanding, we once again said a definite No! to any further personal involvement of a child's natural parents.Why! We asked was this social worker so obsessed with the rights of these often dysfunctional birth families, such families children were often in the care system because of the way their parents were behaving or because of the way that they were bringing up their children, we certainly would not have wanted any involvement with people who have chosen a wayward form of lifestyle and for these people to be involved in decisions taken regarding a child that we were about to adopt.

Many social workers acquiesce in the totally disastrous way of life choices of irresponsible, feckless parents, alcoholics, drug addicts and the like, they need urgently to get them to face up to their problems, it is no good them just acting in the main helping these people to secure services and benefits from the state, the way that many of these parents were behaving promoted abuse, domestic violence, one only has to read many of the recent reports of the way children suffer or even die at the hands of many of these totally irresponsible parents. We could clearly see that it could well lead to all kinds of problems for such people to have any kind of involvement in our lives, if they had tried hard to bring up their children in a good and upright, honourable and loving way, their children might well have still been with them.

What if the child's family were on hard drugs had a criminal or violent lifestyle, or maybe had been physically or mentally abusing their children. When one adopts a child, that child legally becomes the child of that person or persons, there is even a new birth certificate supplied to prove that very point.

If a couple naturally had a child, they would certainly not want, what could well be very unsavoury characters having any knowledge or dealings with their children, adopted children should be treated in the same way.

If all avenues have been exhausted and the welfare of a child is in danger for whatever reason, surely it is better to take the child completely away from the kind of lifestyle the child was currently in, then for the the child to be put into the care system for their own protection and then as soon as humanly possible for the child to be found a new permanent loving home, as any direct contact with the child's past at that point in their lives could, if they come from a bad home with parents who were likely to endanger the child or children in any way, that could if not immediately acted upon be an absolute and utter disaster and could even put that child's life in mortal danger. Surely it would be common sense that the people who eventually adopt a child do not want the added stress of having to worry about the very people who have very likely badly let their own children down. There are enough recent cases in the news of horrendous treatment that some of these dear children suffer at the hands of their natural parents, all kinds of abuse, prolonged torture and even murder, if social services workers had done their job properly it is very likely that these children would still be alive, surely any delays in the adoption process can have a severe impact on the well being, health and development of a child and needs to be prevented if at all possible.

If the children in question wish to see their natural parents when they get older we would be in complete agreement with that providing of course that it was safe for them to do so, because at a later time when they are over 18 years old then it would ultimately be the child's personal decision.

There may be other exceptions, for instance a young girl gets pregnant, has her baby and for whatever reason cannot look after her baby.

I am sure that we can all think of many other situations where due to unforeseen circumstances a person or persons cannot look after their child or children and they are subsequently adopted, then we believe that there could be some form of anonymous contact via social services, to let the mother know just how her baby or child is getting on, we think that this would be a really kind, heart warming, humane, considerate and loving thing to do.

Our Chances Of Adopting A Child Were Ebbing Away

The meetings with the social worker continued going over much of the same material that we had already covered over the past eighteen months, we could see no light at the end of the tunnel, so we decided that because we were getting older, meaning our chances of adopting a child were ebbing away, we had no alternative but to sell our house which we loved and move to a new local authority area, where hopefully we would as a couple be valued and viewed in a different light and eventually fulfil our desire of adopting a child, it was a huge decision for us both to make, however, we were both still very determined to try really hard to adopt a child.

A house and a home were extremely important to us both, but our heartfelt desire to give one of these little children in state care a loving home, did override in our minds any inconvenience that we might personally have to put up with.

Move Number Two

We sold the house and our cottages on the coast in Scotland and moved, having purchased a farm in Wales, it was in a truly breathtaking position, the driveway leading up to the house on either side there were masses of evening primroses all close on a metre high festooned with an abundance of brilliant large yellow flowers, we absolutely loved them.

Facing the front of the house was a very large hill about a quarter of a mile away from the house, with trees, mainly ash and oak growing around the base of the hill and then on almost to the top, the water supply to the house naturally came down in a channel from this hill into a well situated at the rear of the house, from this well it was then pumped back to the house for our use. I didn't know where the water came from until I talked to a private water engineer who was visiting the house in order to check the system out for us, he told me "Jack and Jill went up the hill to fetch a pail of water." I might add that the water tasted like nectar and was as clear as crystal.

At the back of the house about five hundred metres away was a river which went right through our farmland it was about four metres wide but only about fifteen to twenty centimetres deep at its deepest points, one could very easily walk from one bank to the other in rubber boots, we owned over a half a mile of the river bank on both sides, it was full of fish lots of trout and the occasional salmon.

Our first job was to decorate the house from top to bottom, fit a new oil fired central heating boiler, the old one smoked and rattled like an old steam engine, the smell of oil fumes was awful.

We created a big lawn at the back of the house with border flower beds on either side of the lawn, it was going to be a cottage garden style border, we then planted lots of fruit bushes and apple trees forming a small orchard area.

At the front of the house on a large raised earth bank area on the right hand side of the house, I prepared this by digging in lots of horse manure, this was going to be our organic vegetable plot, we were really enjoying ourselves.

We arranged for a local farmer to rent our many fields, he put horse, sheep and cattle in the various fields and fenced off with electric wire fencing enclosures all of which had the most luscious grass growing.

We had a huge barn and the previous owner sold me an ancient tractor and a JCB digger, I had hours of fun driving them around the farm.

I built Hollie a chicken hut with a big run attached for the chickens to scratch around in, Hollie loved her rescued chickens she used to pick them up and give them each in turn a hug, she kept them spotlessly clean and fed and watered them every day, we were rewarded with lots of delicious brown eggs.

Another local farmer came on a regular basis and for few pounds cut all of our many hedges with his tractor and hedge cutter.

The place was now looking good enough, so we thought, that now was the time to get in touch with the local authority social services informing them, that we would like to adopt a child or children, boys or girls, we arranged for them to call the following week.

Also at this time we had three little poodles, Hollie always did love her dogs, but now had this particular love for poodles, their names were Sophie, Emily and Winston and not forgetting our pet cat Sooty, whom we adopted when she turned up one day on our doorstep and never left.

We strongly suspect that she turned up by arriving on a delivery truck as she had the bad habit of jumping into the back of trucks and vans, when they made deliveries to the house, so she could have come from anywhere in the country.

Farms Are Dangerous Places For Children

The morning arrived, it was early, we rushed around straightened the cushions, cut the lawn, the place was looking good, the social worker named Candy Brazen duly arrived, in she came, we said the usual Hello's, then almost immediately she stepped into our conservatory that was overlooking the back of the house, her head went somewhat from side to side in the direction of the river, it was just like she was watching a game of tennis, we were both expecting her to say 'What a lovely view' or something like that, instead she blurted out in an unbelievably shrill loud voice "Is that a river down there" I said "Yes" she then said in an even more loud voice, she was almost screaming, "Rivers are dangerous places for children" to which I replied "You can easily walk across it in rubber boots and I am willing to fence the river frontage on both sides of the river." To which she answered "Farms are dangerous places for children."

Hollie looked at me in amazement, I was immediately thinking that our dreams of adopting a child had once again come to a shuddering halt, for goodness sake how many families with children actually live on farms it must run into tens of thousands if not millions in the UK.

I started to wonder, are social workers planning to round up all of the children who live on farms and stick them all in their dreadful children's care homes or foster them all out, it would have been bureaucracy gone mad, even more red tape than in communist countries, what a very sad place this country is becoming.

My father and my grandfather both had farms, when I was a young lad, I used to help them to muck out the pigs and cattle, ride with my dad on the tractor, in fact I used to help them with any job that needed to be done on the farm. I never came to any harm, one can take precautions, nevertheless, you cannot wrap children in cotton wool.

In fact other things I used to get up to when I was young, I would climb trees and build tree houses swing on old tyres that we would fix on the end of a long rope and attach it to a tree, that used to be great fun.

We used to race our homemade bikes, made out of any old bike bits that we could find from old thrown away scrapped bikes or sometimes people would give us rusty old bikes, we would paint them up in an amazing array of colours, we would then race these bikes around a cycle racing track that we boys dug out all by hand, the track was constructed by us boys on a rough piece of common land that was at the back of the houses where we lived, we would then stage bike races against teams of other lads from adjacent villages who had their own homemade cycle racing tracks, it was rather like speedway racing but all done on our homemade bikes, sometimes there would be what seemed at first sight to be like awful crashes, with a half a dozen bikes all laying mangled in a heap along with the riders of the bikes, but the worse injuries I can remember were a few cuts an bruises.

I suppose that it was not that much different from today, I do not know what social workers think of the current fashion with children especially boys whizzing around at breakneck speeds on their skateboards on these specially built skateboard parks, where the children hurtle up these huge mounds usually at either end of these skateboard parks doing somersaults and all other kinds of crazy antics, if our shallow river was dangerous for children and indeed the farm, I have no idea what Candy Brazen thinks of these modern children's facilities.

On other occasions a group of us lads used to go swimming in a river on the Norfolk Broads almost every day after school or at weekends in the summertime, we would swim out towards a river cruiser which in those days almost invariably had a rowing boat on tow behind, we used to reach up out of the water and grab the back of the rowing boat that would give us a free ride down river, often a journey of around a half a mile or more, until we saw a cruiser coming towards us in the other direction, we would then swim over to that cruiser, catch hold of their towed rowing boat and hitch a lift back to where we started from, the worst thing that could happen was that sometimes we would lose our swimming trunks, they would often be pulled down by the force of the water, some holiday makers would shout at us, but most just smiled and waved at us.

I am not suggesting any youngsters today should do any of these things, the point that I am making is that I am still here, and dozens of us lads back then, used to do this and I am not aware of any of them ever coming to any harm. What did they used to say 'Boys will be Boys!

One can take every precaution possible, but unfortunately it is a fact of life that accidents can and do happen, a tree branch might fall down and hit us on the head, on the other hand it might not, but does that mean we are never going to go for a walk in a wood, with all of the dangers of travelling in a car, we would certainly never get in one of those. If we all kept worrying about dangers that could happen, none of us would ever set foot outside of our homes. In fact having said that, I am told that our homes are one of the most dangerous places for children to be.

Candy Brazen left, saying that she would be in touch, doing a wheelie on the gravel in our driveway as she went.

Over the next few weeks I phoned her office many times to a zero response, she must have been ignoring us because the reply was always that she was out of the office, in fact I was given many promises from staff in her office, that she would contact us but she never did, I even resorted to sending hers many letters, no reply was forthcoming, we were both a bit sad to think that social workers could behave in such an abstruse way showing no deference towards Hollie and myself, we were both brought up to be well mannered and always try hard to treat others in the way that we would like to be treated ourselves, unfortunately the social workers that we had previously dealt with, seemed to have very little idea, what good manners are and the thought of placing children with a loving family, sadly seemed to be the very last thing that they were thinking about, they seemed only interested in ticking their boxes and their future careers.

Hollie and I sat down and had another of our many involved discussions, at first we talked at length about, are we possibly knocking our heads against a brick wall? Was it worth all of the effort? We discussed that the years were going past, fast, bearing in mind we were told that we were too old when we first started out on our journey to adopt a child, it was indeed very frustrating for us both, needless to say it didn't take us long to grit our teeth and agreed that no matter what, we would continue, it was going to take much more than a few irksome, disobliging social workers to stop us from adopting a child.

We could do absolutely nothing about the river, it was there, full stop, even if we had the power to remove it, we wouldn't it was beautiful.

We decided very reluctantly that there was no alternative, if we wanted to adopt a child once again we would have to move house.

It was quite important for us to make the farm as saleable as possible, resulting in us both working exceptionally hard keeping all the mass of hedgerows neatly cut, as the farmer who used to cut the hedges had recently sadly passed away.

We also planted scores of brightly coloured flowers all around the farmhouse, especially more evening primroses, we both love them they self seed and give a vivid splash of yellow in the garden for months, I then planted rose arches using a little red rose, I have no idea what the name of it is, so I call it 'Grandmothers Rose,' we have always planted this rose in the form of arches at every home we have ever lived at, my dad gave me a cutting many years ago, he told me that this rose came from my grandparents farm, it was growing there when he was a boy, so doing a quick calculation it has been in the family for well over eighty years.

I plant these arches so that every time I walk through them, they not only remind me of my dad but also my grandmother and grandfather.

The vegetable garden was at its peak, a positive joy to behold, full of tasty carrots, french beans, cabbages, courgette's and lettuces, also the small orchard that I had planted was forging ahead, in fact everything was looking good enough for us to sell the farm quickly.

Nevertheless, it took us a good eighteen months to sell the farm, we had a whole host of people looking at it and loved it, but most had to sell their own property first, before they would be in a financial position to go ahead with a purchase of the farm. For us it was going to be a bit of a wrench to move as our heart and soul went into the place that we thought might be our forever home.

Life went on much as usual, we had a few holidays visiting friends in various parts of the country, however, most of the time we spent around the farm when one lives in such a beautiful spot, you tends to lose the desire to go away too often.

I would go with Hollie to nearby towns and while she was doing the grocery shopping, I would look in antique shops, garden centres or do-it-yourself shops, we would usually then meet up and have lunch or if the weather was nice have fish and chips in a park, we like to do that, out in the fresh air, surrounded by pretty plants and flowers, watching all the different kinds of birds, I would also make a point of speaking to people usually the elderly, its amazing how many lonely people there are who while away many hours on their own sitting in parks, I have met loads of such people over the years, a little friendly chat helps to break their loneliness for a while.

Many especially the elderly folk often pour their hearts out to you, quite a few that I have had the pleasure of meeting have recently lost their husbands or wives and have often not had anybody who will stop and listen to their many little stories, if we put ourselves in their position like often going home to an empty house, with only a radio of TV as company, it must be awful, I have suggested to many to perhaps think of getting a little pet dog, many have gone away in a happy frame of mind, thinking that this could well be a good idea, I tell them you always have a good friend with a dog as they are always pleased to see you, they don't care if you are a Dustman or a Duke.

We eventually found a buyer they were from the Midlands, they did not want the farm machinery as they were moving from a farm and had all of their own equipment. We managed to sell all of our farm machinery and equipment at an auction going on at an adjacent farm, I asked the auctioneer if I could put all of my farm equipment in his sale, he said "Bring it round boyoo," we will soon shift it for you, it all sold like hot cakes. I was told by one of the buyers, that when a farmer retires or dies, other local farmers go to the sale of their farm machinery and animals in their hundreds and bid high prices in order to help the farmers widow financially or to give them a good retirement present, it was true there were hundreds of farmers present, all arriving in their land rovers, isn't that a truly wonderful gesture within the Welsh farming community, I was deeply touched by this.

The move was going to be relatively easy for us as we were only moving to a local village around twelve miles up the road, the move should also be fairly easy with the removal men doing most of the work.

The big question now was would we be successful at our new house and home in adopting a child. At that point in time, we had absolutely no idea, thus far we had only had dealings with disobliging, rude, social workers, was it actually possible for us to meet a social worker who really in their hearts had the welfare and future prospects of just one of the children in care that they were supposed to be overseeing, would that one child ever be placed with a family who would never let that child down. Was there such a social worker, did one actually exist or were they all tarred with the same brush? we had no idea, however despite all of the discouragement and setbacks we would soldier on, having not lost any of our enthusiasm to adopt a child, our move was going to be an additional exciting journey on our road to try and adopt a child.

Move Number Three

Staying in Wales we then went on to buy a late Victorian house in a small village, the house was perched on the top of a small hill, it had distant views over meadows with a small stream bordered by trees meandering off into the distance, the house which one entered from the road through a huge set of wrought iron gates, then on up a long twisting driveway which was edged by huge trees on either side, in the grounds was a small cottage which was being used as a storage building, there was also a large building built as four horse stables, the main house was surrounded by the most delightful gardens, which were hugely overgrown with brambles and fireweed.

The vendor had bought the run down house to renovate, prior to living in it himself along with his wife, sadly his wife had passed away, and his dream of doing this house up was no longer his passion, his heart was not in it, thus he was particularly keen to sell the house, because of it holding too many memories of his late wife for him. The house needed an awful lot of work doing to it, so it was going to be a labour of love, not only to make it nice for ourselves, but also looking on the positive side for a future son or daughter also.

The brambles and fireweed choking up the grounds were my first job, even so, I was finding the job of cutting them down a daunting task, however, I was fortunate because one of our new neighbours told me about a small farmer in the village who might help, I called round to see him and he was able to call round to help almost immediately, he had an unusual old fashioned cutting machine with a kind of chimney on top and this was being towed by an even more ancient tractor, with a big smile on his face he put this machine into motion and off he roared around the grounds at an incredibly fast pace and to my delight the brambles and fireweed plus anything else in its path were all cut up into thousands of little bits these were then hurled out of this chimney like arrangement on the top, what would have taken me weeks and weeks to clear by hand it was all done in less than a couple of hours, I must say that I was very impressed.

A couple of days later he returned with his vintage tractor, once again with a big broad smile on his face, this time he set to work on ploughing a large area of the grounds this was going to become my vegetable plot and small orchard area, once again what would have taken me many hours of hard work was all done in a flash.

On the other side of the house was what I called on arrival the bottom garden, we renamed this area the secret garden, as it was down a steep incline and was hugely overgrown, it very obviously had not had any attention in many years, the smiling man with his fabulous old cutting machine was not able to clear this area, as it would have been far too dangerous, this would be a hand job for me in the future.

It took us both many months of hard work to bring the house up to a reasonable standard, painting and decorating, repairs, new kitchen, new curtains and carpets plus a whole host of other jobs.

We Are Desperately Looking For People To Adopt Older Children

At this time we had just about completed most of the renovations to the house, when an advertisement appeared in the local newspaper put in by the well known adoption agency Barnardo's who used to be renowned for looking after boys, the advertisement read like this 'We are desperately looking for people to adopt older children whose needs are complex and often difficult and challenging', a following newspaper news item then highlighted, 'Barnardo's has made a desperate appeal for couples to come forward, as they are battling a shortage of adoptive parents,' it went on by saying 'Prospective parents are vetted by experts? Parents can be from all walks of life, They just have to be committed!'

That was us!, Was this it! We thought, we were now much older, did we feel that we could adopt an older child with difficult and challenging behaviour problems? Having throughout our lives dealt with tens of thousands of people from all walks of life, often dealing with their many problems, we both thought that we had handled and helped to sort out most situations in other peoples lives, especially when running the holiday agency, where we had to deal with, bed wetting, damage to property, people leaving holiday homes filthy, people on holiday would often get extremely angry with us especially if it rained during their holiday, almost every day of the week something would crop up, so dealing with other peoples problems was second nature to us.

Therefore we decided that we may well be good candidates to adopt a difficult child, and there was certainly no doubt's whatsoever that we would be committed,. We decided with a confident 'Yes!' Let us go for it! We were also reading in other reports that there was a huge shortage of people like us, who were prepared to adopt older, hard to place children, maybe then, as there was a huge shortage of people like us, we might then stand a very good chance to adopt a child, don't hold your breath. We duly made an appointment.

The day arrived a couple of project workers from Barnardo's agency, a manager and his assistant were at our front door, then after normal greetings and hello's, we duly showed them around our home finishing up in our lounge, they sat down and we then started to talk about various things connected with adoption for what must have been for about ten minutes, then suddenly the door of the lounge shot open with a quite loud bang and in rushed our three pet poodles, Emily, Winston and Sophie, they usually got excited when greeting visitors to our home, likewise people love all of the excitement of meeting them and make a fuss of them, I called them our hooligans, however, on this occasion it was a little bit different, I have never before or since ever seen anybody jump so high out of their seat, this manager chap just literally leapt up into the air Aaaahhh!, Ooohhh! He blurted out. I thought silently to myself, 'Well that's a good start. Trying enormously hard not to laugh.

Then composing himself this manager started to stare around the room very intently, looking in particular at the corners and cornices of the ceilings and the tops of the walls, he craned his neck around rather like a bird, he continued to gaze around the room, not saying anything, I immediately thought that he might be looking for spiders and their cobwebs or even mould caused by condensation, I knew he wouldn't find any, he then said, rather sternly,"Its a bit clean and tidy isn't it!" to which Hollie said to him. "I like to keep the house clean"
At that point this manager chap then said he would have to leave and he would then be sending us a letter explaining what their thoughts were.

So their flying visit was all over in less than thirty minutes, their fleeting, brief so-called assessment was over, this Barnardo's manager and his assistant had left, leaving us both thinking that if they were genuinely desperately looking for people to adopt these extremely vulnerable hard to place children, they at least ought to give more time and serious thought to the hopeless plight that most of these youngsters were in, rather than our home being clean and tidy. I am not a gambling man, but I would not mind betting that a good many, if not all of these young people might well like to live in a clean and tidy home, A letter duly arrived some weeks later it stated as follows:-

Dear Mr and Mrs Speed
Thank you for the meeting with my assistant and myself the other week, in connection with your interest in adoption through this agency. We have now had the chance to discuss our visit with the rest of the adoption team and I am writing to let you know the outcome of that meeting. Together we felt that you both had a real interest in the well being of children and your wish to offer a home to a child was explained in a genuine and honest way.

However, we need to balance this with our knowledge of the background experiences of the older children we are trying to help and given the complex, difficult and challenging behaviour shown by these children, we do not feel able to invite you to apply to this project. As my assistant and I explained this agency is working with some of the most emotionally damaged children in Wales and we do need to take fully into account the likely behaviour of such children and the potential effect this may have on any adoptive family. I am sorry not to be able to take your interest in adoption further, and would thank you again for your hospitality.

Yours Sincerely

So that was it, our attempt to adopt a child had once again come to a shuddering halt. Not at all deterred or put off, but rather perhaps it made us even more determined to adopt a child, mainly because of this Barnardo's agency advertisement, do you remember?

'We are desperately looking for people to adopt older children'

and we were also very aware that there were literally tens of thousands of children in care, there just had to be just one little person out there who we could adopt who would appreciate a clean and wholesome place to live. Even so, this meeting with this Barnardo's chap, did bring it home to us that time was now not on our side, some eight years had passed since our first meetings with social worker Christine Strange in Scotland.

Many years later we again contacted Barnardo's by letter, as we were never happy by the way they conducted their assessment, we were thinking about other people who planned to adopt, would they also suffer the same problems that we had, you can read all about this later in our story.

I even sent a letter to the Prime Minister of the time explaining the problems that we were having with local authority social services, however, there was not any joy there, the reply letter sent to me was not from the Prime Minister personally, they never are, it came from The Department Of Health, the letter read as follows:-

Dear Mr Speed

Thank you for your letter to the Prime Minister concerning your wish to adopt a child, the Prime Minister has asked me to reply and I apologise for the delay in doing so, I am sorry to hear of the problems you have been experiencing and I can understand your frustration. The government wishes to make the adoption service more sensitive to the needs of the people involved in the process, to make it more efficient and streamlined and to remove any unnecessary obstacles in the current procedures. The adoption review is now complete and the teams report was recently

issued as a consultation document and would welcome your comments on the recommendations. You should address any concerns to the National Assembly of Wales who are responsible for their local authorities.
Yours Sincerely
The Consultation document was a sizeable bound volume absolutely full of jargon all about what they hoped to do, since that time nothing appears to have improved one iota, I don't know about streamlining the system and removing unnecessary obstacles, in fact the whole adoption system subsequently went from bad to worse.

You Couldn't Make It Up

Following the letter writers suggestion, I sent a letter to the National Assembly of Wales, what did they do? In their reply letter to me they told me to go back to my local authority, a real stitch up of pass the paper round, merry- go- round. You Couldn't Make It Up!

Nothing changes, I am just reading in a news report, this member of parliament comments' The state will invest one hundred and fifty million pounds in the adoption system to make it work. That is peanuts when they are talking about spending, Forty Two £Billion Pounds! on a train set from London to the Midlands. (And didn't they say that years ago?) That they were going to flash the cash, to find homes for hard to place children, 'Don't Hold Your Breath', if it works great, but in my experience M.Ps talk a lot, often speaking in vague, complicated riddles, what they say is usually a lot of hot air, there is very rarely any real action, at the present time there are still far too many children in care, the figure has in fact remained the same Sixty seven thousand at the last count, despite a succession of government promises to stop the rot.
There are still these thousands and thousands of children languishing either in children's care home or are being fostered, these children urgently need to be members of a forever loving family they need promises from the state in stone, not to be constantly let down on a regular basis by idle promises that never seem to come to any fruition.

Hollie and myself had another of our discussions regarding adoption, and we thought that perhaps it was now time, as we had moved from the farm and no longer had the problem of the river although we did have a small stream and waterfall at the extreme bottom end of our garden unseen from the house. We thought that we might as well contact Candy Brazen from social services again. Being particularly tenacious, I wrote a letter to her office explaining that as the river was no longer a problem, therefore we wished to reapply to adopt a child.

Unexpectedly a reply letter arrived in the post soon afterwards, it was indeed from Candy Brazen, as follows:-

Social Services Dear Mr Speed

Thank you for your recent enquiry; and I apologise for the delay in contacting you. I note from my records that I visited you in January 1998 at your previous address following your request to be considered for fostering. We wrote to you in September 1998 to ascertain whether you were still interested in attending *an introductory training course for foster carers,* but received no reply, as a result your file was closed. If you would like a home visit to discuss the possibility of making an adoption application, I would advise you to telephone the adoption officer Rose Vanity after the 10th of September to make an arrangement.

Yours Sincerely

I noted from this letter, that she stated that a letter was sent to us in September 1998 inviting us to a training course for foster carers, there was certainly not a letter delivered to our house on or near that date, even when we move house we always pay the Post Office to redirect our mail to our new address, in any case we made it quite clear to her on her visit to our home that we wanted to adopt a child. It very clearly shows from her letter that they were quite prepared for social services to train us to foster a child, clearly once trained to have that child live with us on our farm, which in her own words clearly spoken to us was that she 'Considered Farms to be dangerous for children' and also having the river there, that she also considered to be dangerous for children despite my volunteering to fence it on both sides.

That really proves too me one hundred percent, that social workers who work for local authorities, do not want people to adopt children but rather they want to foster them out in order to protect their jobs by shunting these children from foster carer to foster carer, or by sticking them in so- called children's care homes thus ensuring their jobs and careers are always safe, otherwise what other possible reason could there be for social services being prepared to train us to foster a child, then to have them living with us on our, according to them dangerous farm, where this social worker had clearly stated 'Farms were dangerous places for children,' we therefore then could not adopt a child according to them and have them

33

living in exactly the same situation as it would have been for a fostered child on the farm.

It also proves to me that we moved house because of this river and farm, having been considered dangerous to children by this social worker who therefore gave us completely false information, resulting in us moving house unnecessarily, when there was from this latest information no need to move in order to adopt a child, otherwise it makes absolutely no sense, that it would not be safe for us to adopt a child and have them live with us on our farm, however, we could foster a child and have them living on the same farm with us, we were very obviously blatantly deceived by the social worker.

It was not until I started to write this story and read this letter again that I fully realised the enormity of what this social worker had done by just a few words spoken to us at the farm.

Hollie and I had always suspected from our experiences with them, that these social workers who work for local authorities did not want children to be adopted, by the way that they turn down many thousands of couples and individuals who try hard to adopt, we now had the proof that this was the case.

In the year 1974 a total of 22,502 (Twenty two thousand five hundred and two) children were adopted in the United Kingdom of these 5,174   Five thousand one hundred and seventy four) were babies, now bring that up to the year 2010 the total number of children adopted in the United Kingdom was a mere 3,200 (Three thousand two hundred) of these less than 70 (Seventy) were babies.

Its Not Every Woman's God Given Right To Have A Child

It is known that mixed race Asian and black children had to wait three times longer than a white child to be adopted, is it any wonder that many couples are now looking overseas for a child to adopt, in fact we were contemplating going to a far flung country like China, Russia, Pakistan, India in order to adopt a child. It is absolutely crazy that people have to go to all of this trouble and huge expense in order to adopt a child when there are tens of thousands of children in State care in this country.

However, as a result of this recent letter that we had received from social services asking if we would like an appointment to talk to an adoption officer about the possibility of making an adoption application we shelved the idea of searching for a child to adopt from abroad.

In response to the letter that I received from social worker Candy Brazen, I contacted by telephone this adoption officer a Rose Vanity.

An arrangement was made for her to call at our home, she duly arrived and to our surprise as she was walking through our front door with her nose stuck up in the air, giving us the distinct feeling that she was superior to us, we offered her a seat, and before we could say anything, and before she even sat down, the first words out of her mouth in a high pitched loud lordly voice she said,

"Its not every woman's God given right to have a child"

I might add that she was not in our house for very long, this adoption officer was rude and insensitive towards Hollie, we always got on well with the vast majority of people, but this person, I refuse to call her a lady, was by her manner uncaring, tactless, self- important and egotistical, how on earth these uncouth people are given the responsible job of assessing people for the placement of vulnerable children for adoption with loving families, I have absolutely no idea, unfortunately sadly it is the children who ultimately suffer because of people like her with her condescending, impolite, attitude, especially towards Hollie, she left our house in the same way as she had arrived, with her nose high in the air, despite us having yet another disappointment we were both very happy to see the back of her.

Incensed by this Rose Vanity's patronizing attitude and her being in a job that could mean that somebody's chances to adopt a child could be dashed by a few harsh words out of her mouth, I am a person who does not get steamed up easily, but this took the biscuit, I was infuriated, for over nine years Hollie and I had met many local authority social workers, who were definitely without question, not putting the children first, despite them always harping on that they were, we were bending over backwards to offer a child a home, we were not fat, we didn't smoke cigarettes, we didn't sponge off the State, we were both in excellent health, neither of us had ever been in trouble with the law, we do not swear or use any bad language, we do not, nor have we ever, taken drugs, we worked hard all of our lives paying our taxes, we were not bankrupt.

Our first request to adopt a child was now well over nine years ago, what on earth does one have to do we thought, to be able to adopt just one of these vulnerable children? People who are able to have a family of their own are not vetted in this way, they can be middle class, smoke cigarettes, take drugs, never have a job, they can have a criminal background, the list is endless, and with their first child they also have zero knowledge of bringing up a child.

Judging by the criteria set by social services to be able to adopt a child, many of these people would not stand a chance to adopt their own children, so I ask why are their circumstances so remarkably different in the eyes of local authority social workers when it comes to a caring couple wanting to adopt a child?

A recent report stated that of the more than 25,000 (twenty five thousand) couples or individuals who put themselves forward to adopt children in a given year, only around three thousand are approved as prospective parents by social workers to adopt a child that means that a total of typically 22,000 (Twenty two thousand) couples or single people who tried to adopt were disappearing from the system yearly, only a very small amount of people are eventually approved as adoptive parents.

The figures in that given year were of the 65,000 (sixty five thousand) children in care, only just over 3,000 (Three thousand) in that year were adopted from the care system. These figures are an absolute disgrace, it was now very easy for us to see just why Hollie and Myself were being continually being turned down by social services.

The biggest tragedy of all is the thought of tens of thousands of children every year who are left languishing in the care of social services are getting older, therefore that means that they become very much harder to place with a caring family and the amount of the children in this situation increases daily.

I feel that I must highlight all of this absolute nonsense about loving white families not being able to adopt a mixed race, Asian or black child or a black family not being able to adopt a mixed race or white child is wrong. Its the love and care of these children that is vitally important not the colour of their skin.

The law puts it like this: Race discrimination occurs when a person is treated less favourably on the grounds of race, colour, nationality, ethnic or national origin.

This appears to go on all of the time within the adoption system in the United Kingdom, such children in care appear to be treated far less favourably when awaiting adoption, and the prospective adopter's themselves, indeed seem to have the very same problem, by not being able to adopt a child with a different colour skin, therefore it is in my opinion that it is high time that social services, started to obey the law or rules and stop hiding behind this pretence and ill-considered and perhaps law breaking political correctness nonsense that an ethnic /cultural match is necessary for these children, especially as many of these children were no doubt born in the United Kingdom and are therefore British citizens. It is reported that mixed race, black and Asian children in the United Kingdom can wait three times as long as white children to be placed with a loving family, These children are then without a shadow of doubt being treated far less favourably on the grounds of their race, colour, nationality, and ethnic and national origin, that certainly seems to me to be at odds with the law and their human rights, these children do not have a level playing field when it comes to the chance of being adopted. Local Authorities need to stop this nonsense forthwith, after all we are all descendants of a human common ancestor.

Wouldn't it be a remarkably simple and common sense thing to do, for social workers to place mixed race, Asian and black children or indeed children of any nationality already living in this country, born here ,who are very obviously patrial, having every right to live in the United Kingdom through British birth of parents/grandparents, if they are in care and need a forever family to look after them and care for them, forgetting all of this ethnic cultural stuff, they are British and probably love all their baked beans in tomato sauce and their marmite, because without a doubt there are plenty of people who would give their right arm to adopt these children, because of who they are and for the love of these children, not what colour skin they have.

These people prove this very point by searching very often to the ends of the earth searching for such a child or children to adopt.
We therefore desperately need a new law banning this practice of racial discrimination, by hiding behind this cultural and ethnic match business being carried out by local authority social services this uncivilised practice needs very urgently to be outlawed by the law forthwith.
In the United States Of America the law prohibits the denial or delay of a child for adoptive placement on the grounds of colour or national origin.
I am led to believe that there are possibly some new rules from the State coming into force to rectify these disgusting goings on as at present regarding ethnic and cultural differences as used by local authorities social services that is stopping the adoption of such a child that needs loving parents and not forgetting the adopters who wish to adopt these children.

It cannot come soon enough, nobody has the right to make up their own rules that go against the natural and human rights of individuals.
So let us only hope that this business of white middle class, ethnic and cultural differences, colour, age and the host of other absolutely daft

small- minded, spineless ideas as used by social services are shelved forever so that every child in the hands of these social services people are placed as soon as humanly possible in loving homes, with the very people who really do care about what happens to these children.

One Third Of Children In Social Services Care Will In All Probability Never Find A Forever Loving Home

Many people may not be aware that various reports state that over the last few years, hundreds of children have died under social services care, many more are sexually abused, physically abused, in some cases according to recent reports, children are battered, some are starved, one therefore has to ask should local authority social services continue to be responsible to oversee this very important work, as they are very obviously letting down the thousands of children they are supposed to be caring for, they are not learning the lessons!
In fact one could reasonably say that they are not fit for purpose, also it is staggering that it is estimated that around one third of all children in care will in all probability never find a forever loving family to live with, they will either probably end up living with often frequently changing foster carers or they will alternatively end up living in a children's care home, where many, it is said are not cared for in the correct manner, recent reports have alleged that many children in some of these children's care homes have been groomed for sex by gangs of men. The state has repeatedly promised over the years that it is going to sort out this kind of mess, however very little has ever been done to sort it out as recent investigations have shown that one in four of these children's care homes are said to be just adequate or inadequate, that really is not good enough, these vulnerable children deserve the best, they are in these children's care homes mainly because society has let them down.

Get tough in a friendly kind of way, we considered that was going to be the best way forward, we just had to speak out against these exceptionally rude, negative, inequitable and imperious local authority social workers that we had experienced in our trials to try and adopt a child.
Why should people like Hollie and me and no doubt thousands of others like us, who after all have only one desire, to want to give a child a good home, be treated with disdain and disrespect by social services social workers many of whom seem to show a complete lack of care for these vulnerable children, and when it all goes wrong their usual spiel is 'Lessons are to be learnt' how often have we heard that, the facts clearly show that they never seem to learn.

We started by contacting a person who was a senior officer in social services, after this officer had spoken to Hollie and myself at length on the telephone, an arrangement was made and confirmed in a letter for this officer to visit our home, the letter stated as follows:-

Dear Mr Speed
I would confirm that we are treating this matter very seriously and that I would like to discuss in detail all of the details of our efforts to adopt and the constant barriers we had always encounted, then to consider the most suitable way forward.

Yours Sincerely

The day arrived in early 2001, this social worker senior officer a Mr Jacob Jones had arranged in a separate letter to visit our home at ten thirty in the morning, I waited and waited to no avail, it got to one o' clock there was still no sign of Mr Jones, I thought that I had better give him a ring, I managed to get through to him, reminding him that we had an appointment to meet at ten thirty that day at our home he replied, "Err, Umm, Err,Umm" for quite some time, then he said "Can I come now" to which I said " Yes Please," Hollie unfortunately was not able to be present at this crucial meeting, he arrived just after two o clock, despite his being late, I didn't mention a word about it, I remained totally calm, cool and collective, offering him a seat, I then made him a drink and we started talking.
I then immediately found out by talking to this officer that the left hand appeared not to know what the right hand was doing within local authority social services. I told the officer about the river on our farm, I explained that I would have paid whatever the cost was to fence both sides of the river banks, and how the social worker had knocked that on the head, by saying "Farms were dangerous places for children!" I also highlighted how other social workers were downright rude and insensitive towards Hollie and myself.
I then thought that this officer was going to cry, he was certainly deeply upset, surprised and shocked by the way social workers employed by his local authority and under his oversight were treating prospective adoptive parents, we talked in great detail for several hours.
I found this officer to be like a truly refreshing breath of fresh air, when compared against all the bossy, rude, toffee nosed, aloof, overbearing social workers that Hollie and myself had encounted in our quest to adopt a child, as the officer left, I thanked him for listening, he turned to me shook my hand and said in a exceedingly kind humble way,

"I will do something for you Mr Speed," For the first time in around ten years I felt that at long last it might all start to happen.

Seven months went by, I started to think, was I hoodwinked by this officer, as we had been let down by social workers so many times before, I thought surely not, the officer seemed to be so remarkably pleasant and truthful, during my life in business, having met and spoken too many thousands of people, I considered that I was at least a reasonably good judge of character, had I on this occasion dropped a clanger and got it all wrong?
My judgement of people hadn't let me down, in the August of the year 2001 a letter arrived through our front door it stated the following:-

Dear Mr and Mrs Speed
Many apologise for the delay in proceeding with your adoption, we have decided to ask an independent person outside of our organisation as the fairest way forward, I have had some difficulty in securing the said person. I have now got agreement from an agency that they will undertake assessment and we should now be able to move forward fairly quickly, I shall be in touch as soon as I can confirm the exact details, once again my apologise for what must feel like an interminable delay.
Yours Sincerely
Jacob Jones

At long last a positive response from a really honest caring person within social services, it had taken over ten years for us to come this far, even so, we still had a huge mountain to climb, but the steepness of it was now appearing to be levelling out just a teeny bit.
There was then complete silence for a several months, and as Mr Jones had said in his letter that he would be in touch with us as soon as he could confirm the exact details and we should now be able to move forward fairly quickly and we had heard nothing, I thought that I would give him a ring for a progress report.

Adoption Was Not Now On Our Immediate Road Map

I rang and said to the receptionist "Can I speak to Mr Jacob Jones, please," she said "Who?" I again said, "A Mr Jacob Jones Please" the phone went quiet for a couple of minutes, the receptionist then came back on the phone and said. "Oh, I am sorry but he has left, he has gone to work for another authority." I was stumped, speechless, I just said, "Thank you" and put the phone down, shaking my head from side to side, what now, I thought.

I once again sat down and I had a long talk with Hollie, I said to her "We really cannot go on with this adoption business love, it is just not going to happen, "For the first time in the ten years since we had started out on this adoption path, I am sad to say, I gave up! I normally never quit in fact whatever I am doing, I see it out to the end. Unfortunately it seems to me that when dealing with anything connected to the State, whatever party or coalition is in power, it is virtually impossible to win, they promise everything, then take everything away plus more. They seem to always use local authorities as their puppets, to do most of their unsavoury work so that they can pass any blame for their often scatterbrain schemes on to them, so that the State invariably escapes any blame.

In other words they pass the buck.

In my honest opinion they need not be there at all as parliament is just a talking shop, filled up by puppets of the European Union.

A recent report stated, 'Is democracy dying' I think its a bit late for that, 'It is already dead.'

We thought that we had finally won our long tiring battle, in spite of this our conversation ended up on us saying we must be positive, but adoption was not now on our immediate road map, we were putting it on the back burner, we very obviously both felt extremely sad about this situation, but, we had at this moment in time seemingly reached the end of the road .

We concentrated on the house and garden had a few holidays, not giving adoption a second thought, another three months went by.

Then one evening it was around seven thirty, we were sitting watching TV, the telephone rang, I picked it up, a really chirpy, happy sounding voice of a lady rang out "Is that Mr Speed" to which I replied "Yes," thinking quickly in my mind ' Who on earth could that be, as it wasn't a familiar voice to me, she then continued saying, "I am Sandra Good from a Welsh agency for adoption, can I please come and see you and your wife on the twentieth of November at eleven o clock in the morning."

You could have knocked me down with a feather," I said excitedly, "Yes Please," end of conversation. I immediately told Hollie, we were both exceptionally happy, but there was a tinge of apprehension, were our hopes going to be raised yet again, only too come crashing down?

The morning of the arranged appointment day had arrived, we had absolutely no idea what to expect, would this social worker be like all the rest that we had encounted. We saw her car coming up the driveway, she rang the doorbell, we very gingerly opened the door, standing there was a lady with a huge smile on her face, she said "Hollie and Jenson to which we replied "Yes, come on in" we went through to our lounge and we all sat down, she then introduced herself to us both, "Hello to you both, my name is Sandra, Sandra Good, I am a freelance social worker."

This lady turned out to be like an angel without wings, she just oozed out kindness, as we talked she was warm, considerate, thoughtful, attentive, concerned, sympathetic and gracious, in fact she was like a huge breath of fresh air, she said I have been requested to complete a fostering and adoption form on yourselves by the county council, via the agency that I am working for, we were no strangers to this form as we had gone through the selfsame thing years earlier in Scotland.

We talked together for well over four hours, literally getting on like a house on fire, with endless cups of tea, covering every area of our lives. Where we were born? Our parents? Did we have any brothers and sisters? Where we had lived? Our jobs? Our businesses? So much of her visit and talking was covering serious stuff along with some light hearted things with much laughter, she was so unbelievably kind and pleasant, we both found it very hard to take it all in, here in our presence was a social worker who absolutely really did care about vulnerable children who were in State care and she desperately wanted to find them a loving home, quite unlike our previous experiences, we could hardly believe how fortunate we were, at long last we might just be able to adopt a child, we thought?

The time came for Sandra to leave, she lived some seventy miles away from our home, she said ,"I am very sorry but I have to leave because I have a long way to go, so sadly, I had better be off," once again all smiles as she got up and made her way through from the lounge towards our front door, at this point she turned around and for a brief moment said nothing, then she looked Hollie straight in the eye, then turned her eyes straight towards mine, gave a smile, then said to us both, "I like you pair a lot and I will have you a child within three months, we were speechless, astonished, we thought can this really be true, our confidence at that moment was given a huge boost.

We said our goodbyes, still not really believing what we had just heard, Sandra then left, What a lovely gracious lady.

At this point of our journey, we both thought how glad we were to have persevered, we had been through massive ups and downs and at times really felt like walking away from all of the hassle and stress of it all, it would have been very easy to throw in the towel, give up our quest, however, despite the hiccups and disappointments by keeping our eyes on the prize of adopting a child that would be ours, it was looking as if it may now really come true.

It Was Like Winning The Lottery And The Football Pools All Rolled Into One

So all of you out there thousands of you, who have been disappointed, please keep that flame alive, do not give up, it may be enormously hard at times, and as in our case it may take an awful long time to achieve your goal, but as we have found by sheer doggedness and willpower and by being tenacious, unswerving and determined, you will find that there are just a very a few good people who will help you, we met an honest good man Jacob Jones, who has introduced us to this well mannered, polite respectful and wonderful lady, Sandra Good, who is without a doubt a brick, we had complete confidence in her.

We do not doubt for one minute that there are within social services many social workers who really do care about the children and try hard to place children with loving parents, but sadly, regretfully we did not find you to help us, if you are such a helpful person, whose heart is in the right place, the road must be extremely hard for you with all of the political correctness, misguided nonsense and red tape to contend with, it must be a bit of a nightmare for you, however, you must not give up, rather try to improve the awful adoption system from within, the social workers I have referred to who were uncaring and rude, they were quite obviously not you, you know who you are, please continue with your good work as every child in care deserves to be placed with a caring family, and you, yes you! Can make it happen, keep up the good work and I know that your blessings and rewards will give you satisfaction beyond your wildest dreams and those dear children that you continually help, they will until the day that they die, all of them that you have helped, thank you from the bottom of their hearts.

With all of the confidence that we had in Sandra, it sort of seemed like the end of our story, as we were so happy, in actual fact it was really just another beginning, there have been so many beginnings and ends in our story that it all at times seems to be a bit unreal, all of the thousands and thousands of couples like us who want to adopt a child or children are a huge very valuable resource to the State, but somehow they just do not realise or appreciate this, it is a tragedy that they behave in this way, maybe some day they may all understand that these dear people who are often rejected or even treated with disdain, are truly remarkable, special people who are prepared to dedicate often many years of their lives often making huge sacrifices to help a child on their pathway of life, so all of you members of the government and social workers, what do they say nowadays? Get a grip! Please start to appreciate just what a valuable group of people you have at your disposal, I think ' Salt of the Earth' sums them up very nicely. Please, respect such people. Thank you.

About a month had passed since we first met Sandra, once again in the evening the phone rang on picking it up a chirpy voice said, "Hello is that you Jenson, its Sandra Good," she then said, " I have some good news for you, are you ready for this? Do you want to sit down? Are you ready?" I quickly wondered what on earth can she be talking about, do I want to sit down?

She then said," Jenson, there is a beautiful little blue eyed blonde girl, who is desperate for a forever mum and dad are you and Hollie interested, she is seven years old,"she continued " I had this little girl in mind for you both, when we first met." This dear, dear lady, who said she would have us a child within three months, bless her, she had in her mind, a little girl lined up for us, who we can hopefully adopt, right from the time she first met us, to think that she has done all of this in the space of just four weeks for us, in fact it was particularly hard to take it all in, getting on for eleven years of waiting and wondering, would we ever be able to adopt a child, and here we are, now having the possibility of having our very own daughter, it was like winning the lottery and the football pools all rolled into one, in fact it was far better than that, words could not describe how we felt, we could not really express the right words to Sandra, we just said, "Thank you," however, that was really not good enough, a million thank you's could not express our total joy, it was so wonderful.

From then on in it reminded us of Scotland, Sandra would from now on visit us at our home on a regular basis to go through the necessary adoption material, the same meetings with the social worker in Scotland went on for well over eighteen months, we could only hope that these meetings with Sandra could be handled in a bit shorter time, the meetings covered would obviously at the very least take several months and they seem to cover absolutely, everything, things like the following:-
We discussed in great detail, Typically describe your family lifestyle? What would a child in your home experience? Are you open or controlled in expressing feelings? Cuddlers or Touch me not's? Do you do things as a family group or have separate activities? Are you involved with Friend? Neighbours? Church? Clubs? Likes and dislikes? Attitude to money?

Food? Health? Ill health? How important will school be? Homework? Achievements? Are household rules important? Disciplines used? Who decides? Are birthdays and special occasions celebrated? What special roles exist in the family?Are sexual roles important? Is there any stress on femininity for girls, toughness for boys? How would a child fit in your family? Would you accept a child with behaviour problems?

These are just a very small taste of the kinds of questions asked and discussed in detail along with Sandra.

Would You Like To See Her From A Distance

What a huge difference we noticed going through through this along with Sandra, when compared to the experience we had in Scotland, this time although much of the material was serious stuff it was always handled by Sandra in an easy to understand way, sometimes with a bit of humour added, we actually enjoyed the experience.

The meeting just kept on coming and going, then one day after this particular meeting, Sandra said to us, Jenson and Hollie I have something important to tell you, she said, "You know the little girl I mention to you on the telephone a while ago, her name is Lucy, would you like to see her from a distance," we both not really believing what we just heard said a big "Yes Please" Sandra continued, "You are not really supposed to see her just yet, and when you do see her, you must not talk to her, even so, you can have a quick peek when she comes out of school, she will walk right past your parked car."

Still not really believing that we could see this little girl in the flesh for the very first time, was so exciting for us both, we could not thank Sandra enough for arranging this.The all important day duly arrived we met Lucy's foster carer named Molly at a given location, then we parked in this strategic position where she told us to park on the side of the road, just a stones throw from Lucy's school, the foster carers car was parked just in front of us, we were both absolutely over the moon.

A few moments waiting seemed forever, then suddenly there she was a little blonde girl with the most gorgeous huge bright blue eyes like jewels, she stopped for a while along with her foster carer, they were standing right opposite to our car, just few metres away looking into a small stream of water that ran beside the road, then suddenly Lucy turned and looked straight at us and smiled, in her long blonde hair she had some pretty silvery, flower attachments, she was looking just like a little angel, Hollie gripped my hand tightly and said in a soft gentle voice,"Isn't she lovely."

Then to our complete surprise, Lucy's foster carer Molly Sinclair came over to our car and opened the door and said to Lucy, "Lucy, this is Hollie and Jenson, friends of mine, I would like you to meet them" she then said to Lucy, "Would you like to give them a kiss each" which she did a very gentle peck on our cheeks, no words will ever be able to describe this moment which is locked in time, that will be with us forever.

There was yet more to come, off Lucy went back to the foster carers car, a few seconds later Molly came rushing back to our car all out of breath and with a huge smile on her face, she then blurted out incredibly excited saying "I have something to tell you, Lucy has just said to me, *"I would love to have them as my forever mum and dad"* Our hands went up and clutched our mouths and we couldn't hold back the tears flowing from our eyes, if we could have hand picked a little girl there is no way we have chosen a more lovely little person. What a day! Would little Lucy ever become our daughter?
In the month of April 2002 we received the following life changing letter from our adoption agency.

Dear Mr Speed
Your application to become adoptive parents was considered by our panel on the twenty second of April two thousand and two and a recommendation was made to approve your application subject to receipt of satisfactory local authority checks, I am pleased to be able to inform you that satisfactory checks have now been received and the agency has approved your application to become prospective adoptive parents.
Yours Sincerely
This letter was extremely encouraging and highly welcome, we had taken another huge step in the right direction.

It was around this time that social worker Felicity Cool from social services joined us and Sandra our free-lance social worker in the regular meetings at our home, also at about this time we started to have three monthly meetings with a whole host of social workers present, this meeting was also held at our home. There was one interesting thing Felicity Cool despite her having been coming to these meetings a few of times, she would always without exception prior to the meetings telephone us to say that she was lost and would be late and could we give her directions to our house, she would eventually arrive, only to slump her elbows on our dining table put her head down with her hands wrapped behind her head then she would let out a range of sighs and groans, Oooohhh! Ooaahhh! she always seemed to be terribly stressed.

We continued carrying on with these meetings with our two social workers plus we continued on with the larger three monthly meetings.

Another interesting thing was we now started visiting with Sandra the homes of other people who had adopted children to see how they were getting along with their newly adopted child or children, these were quite informative, we would usually sit in their living room and have tea and biscuits and have a real good chat with these different people.

And then the icing on the cake, we were then finally invited by Sandra to visit the home of the foster carer who was looking after Lucy. At last Hollie and me could meet our little Lucy in her current foster home and speak to her face to face, it was like Christmas and Easter both at the same time, we met Sandra at a petrol station cafe had a coffee and a small chat about what we were to expect from our forthcoming visit, we were then on our way, the suspense and excitement of this visit for us both was enormous.

Arriving at the house, we rang the doorbell, Molly Sinclair opened the door and invited us in, we were then introduced to her by Sandra, although we had very briefly met her before outside of Lucy's school, then we once again set eyes on Lucy, she was even more pretty than we remembered and with those big bright blue eyes it was hard to take your eyes off them as she tried to hide herself behind a half opened kitchen door, just her little face looked out occasionally peeking at us, she seemed to be enormously shy, I then said to her, "Hello Lucy, my name is Jenson, Hollie then said to her, "Hello my name is Hollie" we then got this teeny reply from behind this half opened door with Lucy's head facing downwards towards the floor, "Hello,"the ice was broken, within a couple of minutes, out came all manner of dolls, toys and games, we both ended up like children ourselves, I hadn't played with toys kneeling on the floor since I was a lad.

I took some photographs, they were more valuable than gold to us, Lucy then took us upstairs to show us her bedroom, which had pictures that she had drawn on the walls, then it was time to go, we didn't stay long as, Sandra had said, keep it fairly short on our first visit, so we said our goodbyes, much happier than when we arrived. We then thanked Sandra talking to her for a short while on how very pleased we were on the excellent way our first visit to see Lucy had gone, we couldn't wait for our next visit.

Over the following weeks and months we had several more meetings with Lucy, often we would meet at motorway service stations always having social workers along with us, during these visits we were able to get to know Lucy's foster car Molly quite well, However, getting to know Lucy was the real joy, she was becoming less shy towards us.

We would always take her a little present some sweets, a little teddy bear or something like that.

Our visits then the progressed to taking Lucy out, just the three of us, Hollie, Lucy and myself, it felt altogether very much better, without having to be accompanied by two social workers, I remember well our first trip out walking with Hollie one side, Lucy in the middle and me on the other side, both holding Lucy's tiny little hands, we took up the whole footpath, it was a short walk from her foster carers home to a nearby food store which had a cafe adjacent to it, we had drinks and cakes and we were able to chat to Lucy on her own, it was nice, because in the foster carers home, Molly had also an adopted older boy and she was also fostering a baby boy, the noise going on in the house was very often horrendous, with Bob the Builder often booming out from an enormous big as a house television as well as this a children's drum kit would come out, the bashing of these drums would just go on and on every time we visited so the speaking to social workers became nigh on impossible, in addition foster carer Molly smoked an awful lot of cigarettes, almost to the point of chain smoking, we didn't like the idea of Lucy breathing in all of that passive smoke, it was an awful shame that Molly smoked cigarettes as it was very obviously not doing her health any good either as she had a smokers cough, so our little trips out away from the house, could be much more private, quieter and healthier.

Lucy began to get our trust, on the way back to the house after our little trips out we would always call at a child's play area with swings, slide and roundabout. Lucy absolutely loved these simple things, she would swing high into the air with a huge beaming smile on her face, I think we were enjoying it as much as she was.

Hollie and myself wondered how on earth foster carers were allowed to foster children when the carer smoked cigarettes, as Molly always had a cigarette on the go which was a real danger to all those who lived in the house, in fact on one occasion when we called at the house, Molly didn't answer the door, nor the children, we knew she was supposed to be at home as we had made an appointment with her to visit, so we both peeked through the front window of the house and there laid Molly on her settee with a lit cigarette in her hand, she was sound asleep, we thought to ourselves what a terribly dangerous fire risk for her and the fostered children, we were obviously concerned from then on in for the safety of Lucy and the fostered baby boy, social services must have remarkably different rules for people who want to adopt a child than they have for foster carers.

Lucy Can Come To Our Home.
A few months later Sandra Good gave us a telephone call, she said "Hello Jenson, some more good news for you and Hollie, you are going to be able to take Lucy home with you, a sort of pre-adoption trial, it will start by you being able to take her to your home for just one day at a time to start with, then after a while she will be able to stay at your home over the weekends and finally at the end of her school term she will be able to live with you full time." I carried on talking to Sandra for quite some time asking her all the pro's and con's of this arrangement, Sandra made it very clear that we could collect Lucy from her foster carers house and bring her home with us, without the need of a social worker accompanying us for day trips to start with then she could stay for weekends ending up coming with us full time all without the shackles of having to have a social worker watching over us. That was the best news we had heard for a long time.

Coming off the phone, I straight away informed Hollie, she was really excited about the fact Lucy was coming home, we immediately began to have one of our in depth discussions on matters at hand as we now had to face the facts that it was at last really happening, Lucy was going to be part of our family and very soon.

We just loved the thought, it was vital that we had to make a list of jobs that needed to be done and quick, the list seemed endless, the priority was to prepare her room, give it a paint, new carpet, it was going to be great fun preparing a room for our Lucy, we decided on a purple, not necessarily our choice but we did know from hearing Lucy speaking to us that she liked the colour purple, and we did take note that this was the colour of her bedroom walls at Molly's house, so we decided on one of those, what did the advertisement used to say a whiter shade of purple, or in other words a light purple, we had to choose pictures for her bedroom walls, some cuddly toys, we already had a big double bed, we thought that she might like a big bed, we bought a pretty duvet, we already had a wardrobe and dressing table. So we put all of this into action, the finished room after a lot of care and attention to detail was finally ready, and even if I say so myself, it did look pretty good. We both thought that Lucy would like it? We could now pick our Lucy up for the very first time to come and visit our home and indeed her new home.

We called to pick her up at Molly's house, she was ready, looking like a little princess, she got in the car all excited, we were then in conversation and laughter, for the eighty odd mile trip to our home, on the way we stopped at the compulsory swings and roundabouts in a village,

49

Lucy just lapped that up, she loved it, but the big question was, would she like her new home?

On arriving home we thought that we would first of all give Lucy a tour of the house, after introducing her to our three black poodle dogs, Sophie, Winston and Emily and of course not forgetting Sooty the cat, she absolutely loved them all. She then led the way going around the house with us telling her which way to go, we went from room to room, starting with the kitchen, then the lounge, followed by the drawing room, then the bathroom followed by the conservatory, we were going round the house like a dose of salts, Hollie and myself following on behind and the dogs following us all excited barking their little heads off, words can hardly describe the absolute joy of watching this little girls excitement of exploring her new home, the final room we came to was Lucy's bedroom, we said to her "Now this is your bedroom"I opened the door for her, letting her enter the room first, she then turned to face us, her big blue eyes were wide open, it was as if they were lit up and her little mouth was fully open, she then she gave us a big smile, she didn't say anything, she didn't need to her little face said it all.

Next came the tour of the garden, I love gardening and I hoped that Lucy would like it as well, there was over two and a half acres for her to explore including the secret garden, we were as enchanted as she was, just looking a her expressions, she was absolutely enthralled, although I think that she was finding it hard to take it all in, I led her to the top of the secret garden, to get to the bottom I had hand dug scores of steps and fitted a rustic hand rail, I thought that she might find negotiating the steps a bit difficult to manage, to the contrary she managed to walk down them with the greatest of ease, in fact she when down them it a sort of jumping fashion, on the way down we went under a couple of arches planted with grandmothers little red roses, right down to the very bottom, to the streams stepped waterfalls.

I must confess that I never told the social worker that we had a small stream with waterfalls at the bottom of the garden for fear that they would reject this house also, in any case when we bought the house the bottom of this area of garden was inaccessible because of the huge amount of brambles, fireweed, elder, hops, bushes and trees, making the stream and waterfall unseen from the house. When near to the stream it made a trickling water sound, just like music to the ears, I had in preparation for Lucys visit erected a small viewing platform, with a strong safety fence, where she could look over at the waterfalls in complete safety, Lucy stood there for quite a while, she couldn't take her eyes off the waterfall.

We continued on then up another set of steps that I had dug out on the other side of the garden, which took us up and then out of the secret garden this time under arches planted with olearia macrodonta or more commonly know as New Zealand holly this is not used generally for arches, but I use it all of the time, its evergreen and at a certain time of year has the most delightful flowers made up of scores of little daisy like flowers, wonderful! As we came to the top of the steps I had erected a summer house, Lucy just had to have a look inside, she loved it, no doubt having thoughts of being another place for her to play in, we then went round to the paddock bypassing the front of the house where we played ball and had lots of fun, we then had something to eat and drink, however all good things come to an end, as it was time to take Lucy back to her foster carers house, around eighty miles away.

It was great having Lucy staying with us for days to start with and then after a while most weekends, picking Lucy up to be able to stay with us overnight, she would always have with her an overnight little bag and her favourite rather scruffy little doll, despite being a one hundred and sixty mile round trip to pick her up, it was well worth it. Lucy was really opening up talking to us all of the time, we couldn't wait for Lucy to come and live with us permanently when her current school term ended.

Also we knew that Lucy's birthday was coming up in a few weeks time, so I contacted a local garden shed manufacturer who also sold large wooden double swings which in addition had a large yellow slide attachment at one end, we thought that we must buy one of those as a homecoming and birthday present for Lucy, so that is what we did, it came all in bits and pieces like a huge flat pack, it took a bit of erecting as the main frame of the swings were large long pieces of timber which were very heavy, Hollie gave me a hand, we first of all bolted the two ends of the main frame together, each of these ends consisted of two long heavy posts which had to be bolted together in a scissor like fashion with the large main bolts making this scissor fixing approximately 40 centimetres down from the top, these we had to prop up at either end with another two long bits of timber, just to temporarily hold the two ends up, this then enabled us to put the top main cross member to which the swings are eventually attached, up in its permanent position slotted into the two scissor style ends, once that was bolted in position and the temporary props removed, it then began to look like the makings of a double swing.
If it sounds complicated, that was in fact the easy bit, there were masses of bits of timber, support struts, nuts and bolts, washers and screws, if you have ever put a flat pack kitchen unit together it was somewhat like that but on a much grander scale, out of all this lot of bits, we had to construct a box style platform with steps going up to enable children to reach the slide, it took several hours for us to get the whole thing up, all that then

remained was for the two swings to be attached and the slide to be bolted in position. We done this, so it was all systems go, it was looking the part. As we had built this swing and slide Hollie and me felt that we should have the honour of testing it out, it was great fun we were just like a couple of big kids again, although I did find the slide was a bit tight for my bottom.

Lucy's Birthday Party

In addition to all of this we had to find a new school for Lucy to attend a doctor, dentist and a speech therapist, the latter was a real pain as they said that there was no finance available, so I had to go via the government to get that sorted out, after a whole load of bureaucratic nonsense and numerous letters to and from MPs, I finally managed to get a speech therapist, the same applied to Lucy's special needs, we had an awful lot of complications to get this organised, plus we had to deal with all manner of forms that one has to fill in when an extra person newly arrives in your family.

The day arrived it was Lucy's eighth birthday her foster carer Molly arranged to bring her to our home, her car was coming up the driveway, it stopped, out of the car stepped our Lucy, she had an enormously big smile on her face, she looked a real picture, the sweetest little girl one could ever set their eyes on, her long blonde was adorned once again in hair decorations and flowers, she was pushing a kiddies pushchair with her usual scruffy little doll inside neatly covered with a frilly lace cover, I quickly took some photographs, there were then hugs and kisses, followed by laughter. We then all chatting away together proceeded into the house, there was already a party atmosphere as we had invited to the party friends and neighbours children to join us, I had arranged a whole load of games for them all to play in the back garden from an old book of party games, they were those old fashioned games, played with anything one has to hand in fact with many you only need just the children.

I remember as well having fun with marbles, hula hoops, card tricks, pass the parcel, getting them all to dance, face painting and much more, the children were having a whale of a time, laughing every minute.
Hollie had prepared lots to eat, she loves to bake cakes, vegetarian sausage rolls, trifle and a whole load more plus a big birthday cake with the words 'Happy Birthday Lucy,' in icing sugar on the top.
The overriding thing for Hollie and me was that now Lucy was eight years old so it would not be very long before she would be home with us hopefully for good, she was obviously not yet adopted, the sheer joy of having her with us was absolutely fantastic.

We rounded up all of the children and Lucy to come inside and eat all of the goodies that Hollie had prepared, they all tucked in and the party was a huge success, culminating in Lucy opening her presents, however one of the presents she still had not seen, so we called every one present to come round to the front paddock and there stood Lucy's birthday present from Hollie and me, Lucy's new swing and big yellow slide, we had pinned a large brightly coloured banner emblazoned with 'Happy Birthday Lucy', would she like it? You bet, she was on one of the swings in a flash, swinging high into the air, then up the steps down the slide, again and again, then back to the swing, which now had a queue which I also joined, so we ended up with Lucy on one swing and me on the other, I must admit Lucy outshone me yet again, she had this knack of being able to swing breathtakingly high in the air. With all of the children climbing over the swings and slide like ants, I now realised just why it took all of our efforts to erect it using huge bolts, it had to be strong to withstand this onslaught of very happy children.

We then clapped our hands all joining in singing 'Happy Birthday to Lucy,' that brought a tear to our eyes. As the children continued on the swings, I then took the opportunity to take Lucy around the rest of the garden that she didn't have the time to see on her last visit, first we wandered around the vegetable garden, then the orchard area, then we had a look inside the greenhouse followed by a tour of the stables, Lucy loved that, despite us not having any horses, she was fascinated by the taps on the horses drinking cups which were attached to the walls, she always did take an interest in horses, ponies and donkeys wanting to stop at every meadow gateway, if there were animals around.

What a lovely unforgettable day we were having, one of those days that you can look back on and just smile. Sadly all good things unfortunately have to come to an end, Molly was shouting out to Lucy 'Its time to go Lucy,' the look on little Lucy's face just shouted out 'I don't want to go,' these partings became harder and harder for us as we were getting to know Lucy a whole lot better and Lucy desperately wanted us to be her forever mum and dad.

Lucy Didn't Look Back As We Drove Away In The Car

We picked Lucy up for her weekend stays with us a few more times until the day finally arrived, we got the message that we could pick up our Lucy in August to come and live with us as a family, the idea being to see if Lucy was happy living with us and likewise were we going to be happy to adopt Lucy.

This was it! At last! The day had finally arrived for Lucy to come home, we drove to the foster carers house, Lucy was waiting at the door with all of her worldly goods, a sizeable bag of cloths some dolls, teddy bears and other toys and games, social worker Felicity Cool was on hand to oversee the procedure with her note pad in her hand, we gently piled all of Lucy's possessions into the boot of our car, Lucy said her goodbyes, she then shed a tear, Felicity Cool then made the comment, "I don't know why she is crying," well we did, Lucy was obviously very fond of Molly having been with her for over three years, social services had previously moved Lucy from pillar to post, she also, having been taken from her birth parents years earlier, and rightly so.

At the time Lucy was just two over two years old and she still has vivid memories of that day, there were police, and several social workers who removed her from her parents home because of filthy living conditions and severe neglect, we were informed that at the time of her removal there was dog mess all over her clothing. However Lucy would not have fully understood jut what was going on.

So on this occasion it was patently obvious that Lucy was upset, she was on the move yet again, at that precise moment she was very likely deeply concerned about her future, was she perhaps thinking that this was just another temporary move, it would be a traumatic experience for a grown up person let alone a young girl. Like when people move house it can be an awfully stressful time for some people, Lucy wasn't to know that Hollie and myself would never ever let her down, no matter what the circumstances as long as we both had breath in our bodies we would care for her and even if we were to die, we would see to it that she would be cared for by some of our trusted friends to look after her. She wanted a forever mum and dad and we would see to it that is what she was going to get, Lucy bless her heart didn't really know that.

Lucy didn't look back as we drove away in the car, she didn't say anything, in fact she had a deep sulk on her face which we hadn't seen before, I then thought I know what I will do, I will take her to the swings and slide as we were about to drive past a wonderful park, we had visited this park before with Lucy and she really liked it, it was certainly one of the best we had visited, it had an extremely long slide built into the side of a very high mound of earth, from the top of the slide it snaked down many bends to the bottom, that did the trick, Lucy went up to the top and then came hurtling down to the bottom as we were watching, the smile returned to her little face, she did that a couple of times then we all had a swing then it was time to go, that little detour took her mind off what must have been a remarkably happy yet worrying and traumatic day for a little girl, it was not long on the journey home before Lucy was right back to being her old self again, as usual we talked, sang lots of songs it soon took her mind off the earlier upset of the day. Little did Hollie and myself realise that the road ahead in this adoption process was going to be a long gruelling one, but the most important thing at that point in time was that we now had a little girl named Lucy safely in our care.

As the days went by, it was not all roses, Lucy had fairly constant bad tantrums, she would stamp her little feet and try and get her own way, Molly had warned us that she had a little bad temper.
Lucy also had problems in other ways for instance, if Hollie or myself stepped outside in the garden for just a brief moment or into another room in the house or even just going upstairs and Lucy couldn't find us, she would let out a huge scream at the top of her voice "Where are you dad? Where are you? Where are you?" the same with mum, she would give the same screams "Where are you mum? Where are you?" She was absolutely petrified of being left alone for more than a few brief seconds.
If I ever had to take Lucy out with me without Hollie, into a Town shopping or to go to the bank, it presented problems, if I wanted to go to the toilet, I would say to Lucy "Now wait there, I will only be a moment," having just got through the toilet door, I would hear those very familiar words scream out "Where are you dad? Where are you?" Within seconds she would be inside the gents toilet.

As the weeks turned into months, Lucy slowly but surely realised that we were not going to leave her, also her bad mood tantrums began to get a bit less in number, however on one occasion that clearly comes to mind, we were in a small seaside holiday town in Wales. Hollie went off on her own to do some food shopping, I took Lucy into a shop come cafe, it was packed with customers, we both sat down at a table and had drinks, Lucy's eye spotted some rather enormous plastic windmills, she wanted one, I said "No! Lucy, they are far too big to get in the car," she wanted one and would not take No! For an answer, she was screaming at the top of her voice," I want one!, I want one!. I must admit it was a trifle embarrassing, she got up from the table and started stamping her little feet, everybody was looking at us, I wouldn't mind betting that they were all thinking what a badly behave child, I felt awkward, should I buy her one to keep the peace? I might add, I didn't, Lucy had to learn that it is not possible to have everything that she wants.

I always remember our dear departed friend Tom, he had a little saying that I always keep in mind, 'Happiness is not having what you want, but wanting what you have.'

At bedtime we would take it in turns to read a bedtime story to Lucy and we would also often have a sing song with her, at first she wouldn't join in however one could see her little lips moving just a bit in tune with the song, however, after a few weeks Lucy had started to join in, I clearly remember us singing together lots of popular children's songs, Lucy loved to sing those songs, plus many more, singing along with us at the top of her little voice.

Hollie worked really hard in helping Lucy to read and telling the time took forever, Lucy just could not get the hang of it, but, Hollie persisted the reward finally came after months and months of help Lucy finally cracked it and was able to tell the time. Lucy had to get used to lots of new things quite quickly, she attended a new school, which she was finding quite difficult, it was a Welsh speaking school resulting in her not knowing or understanding what the teachers announced, or even understanding which classroom she was meant to go in, it was proving to be immensely difficult for her.   On one occasion Lucy came home from school and complained to us that she couldn't see the items written on the blackboard, here was a little girl eight years old and no one from social services, nor her foster carer had thought to get her eyes tested, we very promptly did this resulting in Lucy being prescribed glasses, it was exceptionally annoying because the   optician informed us that she had lazy eye, which if treated when a child is younger it apparently could have been cured, however he said that it was now not possible to cure the problem in Lucy's case, even so, the glasses helped Lucy enormously.

We had also been informed that Lucy had been deaf for the first few years of her life, it was now very obvious to us, what with her not being able to hear and not being able to see clearly, this was the reason why she had difficulty in learning new things, although her hearing had been corrected with a minor operation, it was now clear that is why she was way behind other children of her age, with the poor little girl having hearing problems and sight problems it was quite obvious that her learning new things greatly suffered. In fact on coming to live with us at almost eight years of age she could only say A.B.C. And count too eleven, she was also special needs and she was having regular speech therapy with a specialist teacher, in particular with a focus on phonology, speech patterns and syntax, in fact at times Hollie and myself would sometimes struggle to understand what Lucy was saying, that used to make Lucy mad.

Lucy now being in our care and hopefully she would soon be out of the hands of social services. We taught her almost everything that we had come to know, being determined to give her every bit of help that we possibly could, carefully, slowly and gently without overloading her, we started to teach her math's, how to read and write, we made homemade birthday and greetings cards with her, we taught her how to speak in a proper manner, in fact within a period of around six months her speech therapy teacher said to us "I do not need to see Lucy anymore, you have both done wonders for her, Thank you very much."

Lucy Continued To Blossom

It took Hollie and myself hours and hours and hours of patient gentle persuasion to get Lucy to want to learn new things, she had what social services called a short attention span, our help and guidence was only then just beginning to pay off, Lucy continued to blossom and she was now slowly beginning to enjoy it.We taught her about the wonderful world all around us, it was lovely to see her in the garden, she had her very own little patch to look after where she planted all kinds of flowers, she even started to take an interest in seed catalogues asking us many questions about what seeds to plant, where and when to plant them, that really impressed me. She loved to watch the birds in the garden or in the countryside when we were out walking, she began to recognise many of them, she got to know with our help the Great Tit, Blue Tit, Long Tailed Tit, Robin, Blackbird, Jay, Ring Dove, Pheasant and many more, she would often rush into the house all excited and say, "Quick dad, what's the name of that bird?" What a little twitcher! It was the same with butterflies, she could recognise and name, Tortoiseshells, Peacocks, Red Admirals and many more.

She even started to read the daily newspaper, in fact that was where we were seeing the most progress, she loved to read, coming home from school, she would every day say, "Can I please have a chocolate and where is the newspaper?" Notice this little girl would never take a sweet or a chocolate without first saying to Hollie or myself, "Please, can I please have this or that," and once we said "Yes" she would always say "Thankyou" That really impressed us both, her manners, in fact if at times when she didn't hear us correctly, she would always say "Pardon."

We would constantly get little notes from her, especially if we told her off for anything, a little note would suddenly appear usually with a little drawing of a cat or a dog, sometimes a flower or a matchstick drawing of mum and dad on a little scrap of paper, it would say something like, 'I am sorry for what I did,' underneath that it would usually say, 'Love you lots and lots and lots' followed by around 20 kisses xxxxxxxxxx.
It was becoming noticeably obvious to us that our little girl Lucy was beginning to turn out to be a little treasure, she was particularly well

mannered and was quickly losing her fear of being left alone and she was now truly eager to learn new things, and from her little notes she showed that had really bonded with us, respected us and loved us.

She would every day take the dogs around the secret garden always taking with her the dogs poo bags, she would pick up the dog waste and deposit it in the correct bin, she done this as a matter of routine.
She got on unbelievably well with the dogs and the cat Sooty, in fact they became her little mates, we would often hear her in the garden giving them their instructions, sit, shake hands, orders not to pull on their leads, the dogs were exceptionally good with her they took it all in their stride, she loved them and they loved her, they were her little friends, she would often tell us that she loved them. It was strange thinking back Lucy had said to her foster carer Molly that she would like to live with a forever mum and dad who had a motorhome which Lucy called 'A house on wheels,' and two dogs, that was us, in fact we went one better having a house on wheels and three dogs and a cat and Lucy always did tell us that she had chosen us.

Regarding the motorhome, I remember well not long after Lucy arrived we planned our first holiday with her, we discussed with her which location she would like to visit and we came to the unanimous decision, a place called Bala lake not far from Mount Snowdon, I remember saying to Lucy when showing her the layout of the motorhome, pointing to the big double bed up above the drivers cab with a wooden ladder to gain access, I said to her "That's your bed up there" I got a very stern reply "I am not going up there," I replied "Right, we will not be going on holiday then," in a flash Lucy then shot up the ladder and laid down on the bed saying "Its nice up here dad, I like it."

Cold Wind Bay I Am Not Going There It Will Be Cold There

The campsite at Bala was close to the lake and was surrounded by a backdrop of woodland, it was really pretty, just the same Lucy seemed to be enormously nervous of everything, she was nervous being near the lake, she kept on saying, "What's that noise" the slightest ripple in the water like a fish jumping up to catch a fly really scared her and she was terrified just to walk along a path adjacent to the woodland and if a small branch of a tree or leaf touched her face, she would shake with fear, however, we did have our good times on that holiday visiting the local village which was very pleasant, it was situated on the opposite side of the lake to the campsite, we had several meals there in some excellent restaurants and cafes plus we visited Mount Snowdon and lots of other interesting places.

On arriving home, I telephoned Sandra to tell her about Lucy being so nervous when she was near the lake or near the woodland.

Sandra informed me that her foster carer Molly very rarely took her out of the house which was in a built up area, when she did take her out it would only be to the shops which invariably would always be in a town, so poor Lucy was not at all familiar with going into the countryside and it would all have been a totally new experience for her. It was a great pity because despite us comforting her, she was extremely wary of many things throughout that first holiday with us.

Our next holiday was to Colwyn Bay, again we discussed the holiday as a family, Hollie commented,"I think it will be nice there and I haven't been to Colwyn Bay before," Lucy then said very sternly, "I am not going there, Cold Wind Bay, it will be cold there," after explaining to her that it was Colwyn Bay and it was no colder than anywhere else, she agreed that she would like to go on a holiday there.

So a few weeks later we ventured up to a camp site not far from Colwyn Bay, the site which we pre-booked was immediately adjacent to the main railway line to Hollyhead, the receptionist said, "I have booked you in on a pitch over there" pointing towards the railway line, I protested and he said; "Alright you can have a pitch over near the hedge on the far side," this was well away from the railway track, so it was agreed, we set up with chocks, organised the electricity and water supply, sorted out the gas and started our holiday, it was good, we then all sat down and discussed our holiday plans for the week over a freshly brewed cup of tea, we didn't bother to do any cooking in the motorhome that day, I went and got some fish and chips we then watched a bit of television followed by an early night.

The very next day Lucy said to me dad, "I would love to be over there near the railway track so that I could watch the trains going past," like any new dad, I said to Lucy, that I would ask the receptionist if we could move a bit nearer to the railway track, I duly done this, he didn't seem to be very pleased, he mumbled away to himself, as we had the day before asked to be put somewhere well away from the railway line, however with my charm and gentle persuasion and with Lucy's big blue eyed look, he stuck us right beside the main line.

He probably thought that I had taken leave of my senses, we ended up being parked right beside what must have been one of the busiest railway tracks in the country, it turned out to be horrendous, a high speed train would speed through, followed shortly afterwards by a rumbling goods train the length of which I had never before encounted in my lifetime, a short while later another high speed train would hurtle through at break neck speed in the opposite direction, the wind created by these trains caused the motorhome too sway from side to side and the vibration made the motorhome jump up and down, this continued way into the night, it was a bit like being on a fairground ride.

Here Comes Another One Dad

Lucy would count the trains and she would jump up and down saying "Here comes another one dad" she was absolutely loving it.
Despite the trains which 'Tongue in cheek,' we got used too! It turned out to be a fine holiday area, lots of fun, the beach was just a stones throw away, and there were plenty of them as it was a stony beach, nevertheless, enjoyable, there were lots of different seabirds that we watched, also we went on some very pleasant walks inland, we also visited the Town.
Lucy, after picking up some advertising leaflets and going through them, asked me if we could go along the coast to the seaside town of Rhyl as she had decided that she would like to go for a swim in the Leisure Centre there, although at the time she had no idea on how to swim.
Hollie decided to give it a miss and be a spectator, so Lucy and myself got changed and in we went into the water, I helped Lucy to try and swim and we splashed around, she got great fun out of splashing dad, then after a while there was this huge crack, of manmade thunder, then suddenly it started to pour with rain heavily, this was also manmade and it was cold, then there was a loud hooter type of noise this unbeknown to us was a warning that a huge manmade wave was on its way, it hurtled towards the pair of us, I managed to stay on my feet, just, but poor Lucy was swamped by it and disappeared under the water, like any dexterous brave dad I quickly rescued Lucy by grabbing hold of her, Lucy looked very wet and bedraggled, she immediately couldn't wait to get out of that place.

On another holiday in the motorhome we went up to Scotland, starting off at a site near Balmoral, We didn't see her! (The Queen) Lucy loved every minute of this holiday, she had by now, got used to walking in woodland, forests and beside rivers and lakes, we always took along with us Winston, Emily and Sophie, Lucy loved her little mates coming along with us, the walks with the dogs in Scotland were often along pretty paths through breathtaking scenery which often changed dramatically as we rounded each and every bend.

We visited the City of Aberdeen, they call it Granite City, you can see why when one visits its choc- a- block with lots of lovely granite buildings, we visited a large park near to the city centre, which had masses of glass houses, each one housing differing tropical plants and cacti from all around the world, there were also pretty fish swimming around in the many pools of water, we found one where the fish liked their backs tickled Lucy loved that. We had a meal there in the restaurant that was very enjoyable. I couldn't resist buying a plant, I came away with a couple of aloe vera plants to add to my conservatory collection of plant, we use the jelly from the plant for sun burnt skin and minor burns as it has a cooling effect, we find that it can also be used for eczema and the neutralization of scars.

We then went on to visit Inverness that was nice, then we went to the Black Isle. On the way we stopped at a popular roadside place which has a steep cliff with steps leading down to the sea, it is one of the best places to watch dolphins jump high out of the water, as we watched there were at times two or three of them jumping in liaison in an outstanding display, that was really worth stopping for.

We continued our journey on to the Black Isle that was very pretty, it is not an island at all but rather an area of land jutting out into the sea, I am lead to believe that it got the name Black Isle because the surrounding inland countryside often got lots of snow, hence white, and the Black Isle because of it sticking out into the sea usually got much less snow, so obviously it is not then white. Old wives tale? I do not know.

Lucy then decided that she wanted to see the monster at Loch Ness, we didn't see it, just some waves that tricked our eyes into thinking that we could see a snake like monster, even so we loved the area.

In between these holidays life went on at the house much as usual, Lucy was attending her school, she didn't like it and we were not very happy with her being there.

The meetings with the two social workers were still going ahead as usual, Felicity Cool was still losing herself when attempting to find our home, she would still come in our house and hold her head in the usual fashion and Sandra Good would also be in attendance along with Hollie and myself, these meetings continued on for several months, during which time we discussed the looking after children, and we still had the larger meetings which took place every three months when there were lots of social workers in attendance at our home, at this meeting we would usually go through a consultation paper which was sent to our home prior to the meeting, one for us as future parents and one for Lucy to fill in, they were identical papers with just a different names written on them.

On one occasion that I remember well at one of these meetings, the chair-person came in to our home with a number of other official looking people from social services, they all had either their brief cases or these leather underarm type folders, they all sat down.

Lucy was also in attendance at this meeting it was quite early on as Lucy hadn't been with us very long, although at that time she had progressed quite a bit, but certainly not enough to fill in her copy of this consultation paper, resulting in my filling in Lucy's paper, in fact I still have the original copy of that paper, we were all sitting on chairs arranged in a circle in the middle of our lounge, when this lady chairperson whom I had never met before, said in an unusually snooty posh voice towards me "I see that Lucy didn't fill in her own consultation paper and you took the liberty of filling in her copy for her," it was patently obvious to me at that moment that she had very little knowledge of Lucy's past, nor had she taken the time and trouble to find out more about Lucy prior to this meeting, otherwise she would have known that Lucy was incapable of filling in her copy of this paper.

This resulted in my explaining to her that Lucy on coming to us could only say A.B.C. And count to eleven, "Mmmmm" she said. I notice from my notes which I had written on my copy of the duplicate consultation paper, which I then relayed to her about the first question on the paper, the question was 'How is she doing' my answer was, 'Lucy is eating much better, can now see better now that she has glasses, when she arrived she could only count to eleven, she can now count up too two hundred and thirty and she can now recite the whole alphabet.

These social workers use to really annoy me as they had an almost zero knowledge of the children they were supposed to be overseeing the care of. Especially in Lucy's case for them not to arrange for her eyes to be regularly tested was an utter and total disgrace.

I Decided To Bite My Tongue

On some occasions as many as seven or eight in number of these social workers would throw all kinds of extremely difficult questions at Lucy bombarding her with things that I would have found it difficult to answer, one after the other, question after question, it was hard for me to keep quiet, in any case I decided to always bite my tongue, I thought to myself that Lucy would hopefully soon be out of the hands of this lot, so that is why I kept quiet, although I intensely disliked this kind of interrogation of a little girl.

A letter arrived through our letter box from social services stating that they were not prepared to pay our solicitors legal fees, as they were being charged at a private clients rate, I might add that I had thoroughly researched this and had found out that as Lucy was special needs, a local authority had an obligation to pay most or all of the legal costs involved, this is stated in the British Agencies information booklet entitled 'Adopting a Child' guide.

So be warned! Any of you would be adopters, be alert to solicitors fees and check with the solicitor all the figures in advance, because these fees can run into many, many thousands of pounds, as solicitors can and do often charge two or three hundred pounds per hour, please also note on top of this you will very likely be be responsible to pay the adoption court fees. So it is very wise to check in advance if social services will pay your solicitors bill as it is possible that they will not.

The solicitors letters kept on arriving at a rate of one or two a month, some with good news others extremely depressing, one in particular stated, 'The birth parents have objected to Lucy being adopted and they wish to cancel their care order so that their daughter can return to live with them' we had many similar scare letters, it was like being on a roller coaster in a howling wind, one minute up the next down.
We then received a letter from our agency informing us that due to financial restraints our agency social worker Sandra Good was going to be taken off our case and a new social worker named Brenda Nice would be taking over. Sandra rang us to tell us that she was terribly sorry but it was totally outside of her control that she was going to be taken off our case, she gave us her love and good wishes for the future, we both felt a little bit shattered, she was not just our social worker, she was far more than this, she was also a very dear friend, she meant so much too us, and had done such an awful lot for us, we will both love her forever.
I sent a letter to the head person at the agency as follows:-
Dear Sir,
We have just been informed by letter from yourselves that Sandra Good is no longer going to be our social worker with regard to Lucy the little girl that we are hoping to adopt. My wife Hollie and myself would please ask if you could reconsider this decision as we have now reached a very crucial stage in this adoption process. We are experiencing several problems with Lucy's former foster carer, also meetings have been arranged at which Sandra's presence will be invaluable.
Sandra is particularly familiar with the former foster carer and Lucy, it would be of great concern to us if at this particularly important time this change is made, so we would like to ask you once again if we could please retain the services of Sandra to help us up to the completion of this adoption process, We are both deeply fond of Sandrs and it would mean a great deal to us if you could please arrange this. Thank You.
Yours Sincerely Hollie and Jenson Speed.

The agency telephoned us a few days later to say that it was not possible financially to change this arrangement, but we were not to worry because the new social worker Brenda Nice would look after us.

The problems that we were having with Molly Sinclair, Lucy's former foster carer mentioned in this letter to the agency was that Molly was complaining to the local authority social workers that' She did not think that we would be able to set the right boundaries for Lucy.'

Thinking about it, we were of the opinion that Molly was exceedingly fond of Lucy and had now at this late date suddenly realised that Lucy would no longer be her little fostered daughter, we did feel a deep sadness for her, she was aged around seventy years old and Lucy would in all likelihood probably be the very last little girl that she could foster, I think if she had half a chance she would have liked to adopt Lucy, but, due to her age I doubt that she wouldn't have got over the first hurdle, it must have been hard for Molly. Tossing up between losing Lucy and her thinking these people are going to give her a good home, we guessed how she must have been feeling, because of having Lucy living with us at our home, if Lucy was now taken away we would both have been devastated.

Regarding the agency we need not have worried, true to their word Brenda Nice turned out to be a truly lovely lady, she was a somewhat older lady than Sandra, she struck me as being like a loving, caring mother, we had in fact met her before, she was one of the agency staff who looked after us when we went to one of the agencies training days.

In the days ahead Brenda got on exceedingly well with social worker Felicity Cool, as the meetings continued Felicity mellowed quite a bit she was much more amiable towards Hollie and me, I think that Brenda and Felicity hit it off with each other, there was a definite fondness for each other they seemed as if they could work very well together, and it was now very noticeable that they were both working hard towards a favourable outcome.

Good News! Good New!

Both Hollie and myself now feel that Felicity Cool was earlier under a huge amount of pressure, it was probably that the job was far to much for her to cope with, the paperwork that we had to deal with from her was horrendous, every time we saw her she had her bag stuffed with papers, and after dealing with us, she probably had dealings with other people, I know full well from phoning her office, it seems that she was forever in a meeting of some sort, she had to deal with dozens of solicitors papers, I know that because our solicitor mentioned in several of the letters that they sent to us, they stated that they were urgently awaiting important papers from her social services office.

When we had the holiday business we would always get every last scrap of business bang up to date every day, we allowed nothing to held over to another day, if we had allowed that to happen after a few days we would have had an enormous backlog, that would have put us in a huge muddle. What's the saying 'Don't put off till tomorrow what you can do today.' Poor Felicity appeared to have been making that mistake.

Good News! Good News! At last, from one of the many solicitors letters that arrived through our letter box almost every day now, this was the one we most wanted, we finally had the answer to a huge problem that we were having, the first two lines of the letter stated; 'I write to confirm that I have sight of the report of the guardian and confirmation that the parents of Lucy agree to the proposed adoption. The letter continued on with the best news of all: The final hearing will be in three months time, the hearing will take around fifteen minutes.

Oh Boy! Oh Boy! Oh Boy! What can one possibly say it has taken us from early in the year 1991 to the year 2003 that is a staggering close on thirteen years for Hollie and myself to have a letter in our hands giving us the chance to finally have our very own child a lovely little daughter named Lucy, all that remained was a court case, neither Hollie nor myself have ever been inside a court, but in our minds the first time and hopefully the last will be a pleasant, wonderful life changing experience.

A short time later, Hollie, Lucy and myself met Molly and her grown up son Mark and his future wife at a service station, they lived somewhere near Brighton, when Molly first fostered Lucy, Mark lived at home with Molly, at the time he was just like a big grown up brother to Lucy, he seemed particularly pleased to meet us all especially Lucy, as he had not seen her for close on a couple of years, he then made a real fuss of her, he even picked her up just like a rag doll and held her over his shoulder, I could see his face straining a bit, as she was obviously a lot bigger than when he last met her, we then all had a long conversation with him, mainly about our Lucy, after which he had a heart to heart talk with his mum.

You Have Got To Let Her Go Mum

We all sat down at a large table with bench type seats, coffee was then ordered, Mark was sitting directly opposite to his mum Molly.

He very slowly stretched out his hand across the table and very gently held his mums hand and looking straight into his mums eyes, he said in a kindly soft voice "You have got to let her go mum, these dear people will take good care of her, Lucy's whole future is ahead of her, she might not ever get such a chance again," a tear came into the corner of Molly's eye she wiped it away with her finger, I think that Marks words were having a huge influence on Molly, at that poignant moment she new that it was Lucy's future that she had to think about, she raised a little smile and her lips puckered as she gently bit her lower lip, my goodness it must have been hard for her, to lose her little fostered daughter, its a very sad world out there, one minute you can be up, the next minute your whole world can come crashing down with a huge bump.

That three months waiting for the adoption court final hearing seemed like a lifetime, however as usual we were busy looking after Lucy, during that time we explained to her in great detail everything that was happening, in fact we always did keep her informed and share with her everything that was applicable to her, we now thought that as she was very shortly going to be our daughter, it was important that we should talk to her about her change of name, we first of all asked Lucy if she would like to change her first name or Christian name, " Her reply was a definite No!, I would like to keep my first name Lucy," we both thought that it was good that she wanted to keep her Christian name, although she quickly decided that she would like to change her middle name, we then explained that her Surname or last name would be the same as ours, she liked that.

We were still having meetings with Brenda and Felicity they were both over the moon and extremely pleased with the way that things were going and we were still getting letters from the solicitor, and of course we were both now getting excited.

Probably one of the most important and life changing days of our lives had at last finally arrived, the day of the court case, enabling us to adopt our lovely little Lucy, we all got ready, taking just that little bit of extra time to make ourselves presentable, we then set out in the car and headed towards the court allowing ourselves plenty of time as it was a drive of around seventy miles from our home, we arrived in good time in fact we had the time to visit a cafe, we then found our way to the court car park where we sat for a while capturing our thoughts before we entered the courthouse.

Once inside we found that there were around a dozen or so social workers plus a whole host of other people milling around, we were introduced to loads of people who we had not met before, Felicity was there we had a chat with her, then Brenda arrived as did our solicitor, there was a definite buzz about the place, our solicitor then gave us a tour of the building as she was explaining to us all of the procedures, where we pick up papers afterwards, where we should sit and a rough run-down of the likely happenings, then there was a hush, everyone started to take their places on

66

the rows of bench like seats, we were then invited by our solicitor to sit on the front row of the second lot of seats well back from a sort of stage come platform which had a large carved throne like seat situated in the centre of this stage, it had a huge coat of arms with a unicorn and a lion on it, this was attached to the wall directly above this throne like chair.

The only way that I can describe it is, that it was like a cross between a church and a doctors surgery, it was so quiet that you could here a pin drop, all one could hear was the rustle of peoples clothing and papers that many were carrying as they looked around at the others in attendance.

I Like Carrots And I Like Peas

Then suddenly a door opened at the back of this stage and in came the Judge in his long robe, wig and regalia, he walked over and stood in front of this throne, he paused for a few seconds while looking over his glasses, his head then slowly moved from side to side, he was obviously looking at all in attendance, he then gave a big smile and still looking over his glasses his eyes then went straight towards little Lucy, he then said to her in a soft voice "Lucy, what kind of vegetables do you like?" I immediately thought to myself, Did I hear that correctly? Lucy obviously heard the Judge ok, she replied confidently, in a sweet little voice "I like carrots and I like peas," to which the Judge replied, "I think that you ought to come up here and tell me about these vegetables," Lucy very quickly got to her feet and went up the steps on to this stage and started talking to the Judge, I couldn't hear what they were saying to each other.

The judge then turned his head facing towards me, still with this big smile on his face, he said. "Would you like to take some photographs," I then proceeded to take around twenty photographs, during which time every eye in the house was following me around the courthouse, I am not the worlds best photographer, that was not the important thing, what was important was that I would now have a record of that one off day, that will never ever happen again. I sat down again next to Hollie, the Judge then said in quite a loud voice, "Lucy, would you like to call your new mum and dad up here," Lucy then called us both up, Hollie then turned to look at me, she smiled, we then promptly got to our feet and walked up the steps onto the stage walking up to the judge, who by now had a huge grin on his face, he outstretched his hands towards mine and then clutching my hand in a tight double handshake, he said "The very best of luck old mate" he then greeted Hollie wishing her every success in the future, we thanked him, it was all over. Lucy bless her little heart was at last! Now officially our daughter.

The solicitor told us that judges liked these adoption cases, as they usually had to deal with the more unsavoury side of life, so that cases like ours would bring them a brief period of relief from the more unpleasant cases that they had to deal with, I certainly think that our little Lucy made his day a happy one, without a doubt he helped to make our day one of the happiest days of our lives.

We went into an adjacent office, where we were given a copy of Lucy's new birth certificate which had on it her new middle name and of course her new surname, we were then handed a copy of the adoption order.
Lucy was now officially our daughter and we now had in our hands the documents to prove that fact, the almost thirteen years of our wanting to adopt a child that we could call our own was now a reality, we didn't know whether to laugh or cry, I think that we done a bit of both, our future as a family was ahead of us, just what would it bring?

We thanked everybody and said our goodbyes, left the court, Hollie on one side and me on the other side and our Lucy in the middle, we were both holding and gently squeezing her little hands, we didn't want to lose her now, that was without a doubt the most blessed exciting, life changing moment we were ever likely to have, I remember the tears running down Hollies cheeks and I was as excited as a schoolboy, the trip home was full of talking, laughing, crying and singing, we had at the time absolutely no idea how much our lives were going to change, all we could think of was those glorious moments, the years and years of waiting were a million miles from our thoughts, the future had truly just started. Lucy had now lived with us for a total of around sixteen months and she was great to have around, however as she was now officially our daughter we were now facing the future with a child who was our own, one of our first priorities just had to be her education, Lucy was still finding it extremely difficult at school, despite all of our earnest efforts Lucy was still light years behind other pupils of her age.

I was informed that the Welsh Assembly in their wisdom brought in a ruling that any school that taught the Welsh language to children up to the age of eleven, they would not close that school down, so what did most schools do? They taught Welsh to all of those children in their schools up to the age of eleven years old, this very obviously made it very difficult for Lucy, with almost every one of the children in her school speaking the Welsh language, it was at a time when Lucy was having great difficulties learning English.
I do not know all of the facts as I was obviously not at school with Lucy, but many recent reports have highlighted situations such as Parents of pupils at primary schools in rural Wales have claimed that their children

are being punished by teachers who have insisted that they only use the Welsh language, not just inside the school but also at playtime in the playground.

I must make it abundantly clear that I personally was not aware of these type of comments being given to Lucy, she never said, however, many other parents must have been aware of this going on from the particular comments that they had raised about their experiences.
We were however, a little concerned about Lucy at playtime, where she did comment that most of the children only spoke to her in Welsh, which Lucy had virtually zero knowledge of, she probably knew about half a dozen words, it was very obviously a huge stumbling block for her when trying to make friends with other children, which we always encouraged her to do.

The thought of Lucy having to learn a whole new language at eight years of age and being special needs was in our minds totally out of the question, it seemed completely obvious to us that Lucy had far more important things to be concentrating on for her future education and well being, such as maths, reading, writing and learning English. We did contemplate the idea of Lucy learning at home having private tuition, but then thought that she would be far better off going to school as this would give her a more balanced normal type of child's upbringing, we thought it would be wrong to shelter her from the natural rough and tumble of life.

We personally, I might strongly add, had lots of very good friends in Wales, they were Welsh and were able to speak fluently the Welsh language, however, every one of them always spoke to us in English, we as a family visited many of their homes, having many meals together either at their homes or on days out together, they likewise visited our home on a regular basis for get together's, Lucy would also stopover at our friends homes quite often, and their children did likewise and stayed many times at our home, this did enable Lucy to converse easily with their children who also spoke in English, thus she was able to have some close friends by those means.

Lucy's Education Had To Have A Huge Priority Over All Other Things

We found the Welsh people, those that we knew, without exception to be truly friendly, kind, helpful and honourable, if it were not for the Welsh Assembly making up these daft regulations on what language should or should not be taught in their schools, making it extremely difficult for many children like our Lucy, we would more than likely still be living there as we loved our house, loved the garden loved the area, loved the people.

Having discussed the situation at length over quite a long period as to the best possible solution to the problems of Lucy's schooling, all three of us unanimously agreed was to move house, we really loved our home and we felt a trifle gutted at the thought of having to move, nevertheless, we concluded that Lucy's education had to have a huge priority over all other things, here was a little girl who if she stayed in Wales would probably never be able to speak and grasp the language correctly, in the future she would be looking for a job in Wales, therefore not speaking the language in a proficient manner could well be a huge future burden for her when in competition for jobs against other children who would have the advantage over Lucy of being able to speak fluently the Welsh language.
We couldn't help her as we only spoke a very few words In Welsh, a language that we both found extremely difficult to learn.

One positive thing was, although we had moved house several times in our search for Lucy, this would be the first move for us with Lucy.
We all agreed that as mum and dad had moved originally to Scotland to search for a child to adopt at the start of our journey and had now adopted Lucy, that should be our first priority to return there, we knew that the education system in Scotland was extremely good, Hollie loved Scotland, Lucy had enjoyed her holidays there and I would have moved to Timbuktu if I thought it would be of benefit to Lucy and of course there would be almost zero problems with the language as Scotland is in the main English speaking.
So after a few weeks, I ventured up to Scotland to hunt for a new home, we had decided that we liked the area in which we had previously lived, so that would be my first port of call, I had a good journey, upon arrival I booked into a bed and breakfast establishment from where I started my search. I immediately felt right at home in the area, during the first couple of days I looked at around twenty different houses, I usually do a drive past first and if I like what I see, I then book an appointment to look inside a house and have a good look at the garden, there was nothing that I liked, they were either on busy main roads or near industrial areas or the house just didn't look right. I kept in touch with Hollie and Lucy keeping them up to date on my house search.

I then thought how much we loved the superb coastal area where we had previously owned holiday cottages, sadly we had sold them when we moved to Wales, it brought back memories of our dear departed friend Tom, many years had now passed since he died.

I called in to see his wife, she was enormously pleased to see me and I had so much to tell her, we were able to reminisce and look back talking mainly about dear Tom, she was pleased that we were planning to move back to Scotland.

I then got in the car and went back to those villages where I had taken Tom for the very last time years ealier, very little had changed, except there had been built a couple of those elderly peoples care council buildings, the type where elderly people are overseen by a warden, the elderly folk have their own little home within the building, they were tastefully built on a low level having superb views over the sea and distant hills, there were also a few new bungalows built all of good design, otherwise everything looked almost exactly as I remembered, in fact the villages were even more stunning than my memory was recalling, they still took my breath away by their outstanding beauty. I called in to see an old friend of mine, who still lived in one of the villages, I enjoyed that, he filled me in with the latest goings on in the village, so that was nice, he was not aware of anything suitable for us to buy, so no luck there.

I searched long and hard all around the area there was nothing that I could find that was suitable available on the market, I couldn't blame people for not wanting to move house, nevertheless, my visit was not wasted, I decided at that moment, Yes! I would like to find our family a house and home which was near the sea, I know Hollie inside out, knowing that if I could find a property near the sea she would love it and I was almost sure in my mind that Lucy also would love to live near the sea. I then thought to myself, silly me! what little girl wouldn't like to be near the seaside. I used to sing a song about that when I was a lad in short trousers, the one about being near the sea, as I was driving along, I burst into song once more, I simply loved the idea. That then became my goal for the rest of my searching to try and find a house and home for us all, which had to be beside the sea.

I Immediately Felt Right At Home

I went in estate agent after estate agent, would I ever find what I was looking for, driving along I then came across a fairly large village which I had remembered, having driven through many years previously, at first sight I absolutely loved the look of the place, it struck me as being idyllic, lots of little shops, I stopped the car in the centre of the village, I just had to investigate this place, it had a large hardware shop, garden centre, fishing tackle shop, several restaurants and cafes, petrol station, fish and chip shop, small supermarket, several banks, small cinema, post office, antique shops, hotel, library, large school, the lady in the library told me that the village had scores of listed properties and more importantly the village was right beside the sea, having a harbour full of little fishing boats and an enormously long beautiful sandy beach, what could be more perfect.

Now if I could find a nice house here it would be absolutely superb, I drove the car up and down, around and around thinking would I ever be able to find a house and home in this village, I was beginning to think that I was out of luck then suddenly, there it was right in front of me, a detached Victorian house built of granite, it was currently used as a bed and breakfast establishment, in a quiet road a good distance away from the main road going through the centre of the village, the road that it was on was full of similar sized properties all spaced out nicely with good sized front gardens front and rear, in addition it had an entrance driveway where there was parking for several cars, there was an estate agents for sale board in the front garden.

I parked just around the corner from the house and then set out on foot to explore the surrounding area, a short walk away I found a doctors medical centre, then I came across a children's play area about 800 metres away from the house, I thought to myself Lucy would like that, as I continued walking around I came across an unbelievably well kept school, which was surrounded by well tended lawns and there were pretty flower beds dotted all around, to the rear of the school was a large playing field this was surrounded by avenues of trees, I was beginning to think this is absolutely perfect. I then Proceeded to walk around the village, it felt really great, despite being many hundreds of miles from home, I immediately felt right at home, I called in a few of the shops, had a chat with a number of local people, asking them about the area, they all said that they loved living there, one chap who used to live in Cornwall said the weather is far kinder up here than it ever was in Cornwall, I then had a cup of coffee and something to eat in one of the local cafes, then relaxed for a while on a bench seat in the centre of the village in order for my mind to take it all in, then back to the house.

My first job was to look at the garden, that was easy because a narrow no through road went up the side of the house towards the back, the garden was more than perfect it was totally surrounded by a six foot high thick granite wall, a gardeners dream, I visualised planting apple, plum and pear trees planted in such a way to grow against the wall in an espalier or cordon fashion attached to wires fixed along the walls, the walls would keep them sheltered and warm acting like a radiator picking up heat from the sun in the daytime slowly releasing the heat at night protecting trees and plants from any frosts, there was also a greenhouse the style that leaned against the house, these greenhouses are ideal as they pick up warmth from the house, thus keeping the greenhouse inside temperature above freezing, I could see us as a family living there without even stepping inside the house.

I arranged with the estate agent to have a look at the inside of the property, it did not disappoint me, it had high ceilings with elaborate coving's, lovely big rooms, a huge kitchen with a large Aga cooker, being a bed and breakfast business it also had either en-suites or wash hand basins in the bedrooms, it had the most gorgeous mahogany staircase, as I was walking around the house taking it all in, at the same time saying silently to myself Hollie and Lucy would love it here.
The owner of the house was on the brink of purchasing another house, so he was obviously keen to sell, all I had to do now was to telephone Hollie and Lucy.

I Came Away From The School With A Hop A Skip And A Jump

I had in the past purchased a number of properties without Hollie ever having sight of them, she had always liked the houses that I had chosen, being together for many years we had grown to like similar things.
I excitedly phoned them, Hollie as she usual does said "If you think that it is suitable, go for it," I then asked Lucy what she thought, she was more excited than I was, it was quite obvious that she would move anywhere in the world as long as she was with us.

I then proceeded to do a more in depth thorough research of the village and its advantages and any disadvantages if any, I first of all walked up to the school, this was a top priority as that was the sole reason for our moving house and area to get a better education for our Lucy, on arriving at the school, I asked a lady if I could possibly have a word with the head teacher.

I was in luck, she was able to see me there and then, inviting me into her office, she turned out to be a gem of a lady, we both sat down, I then explained to her the difficulties that Lucy was having with her learning in Wales also that she was registered as special needs, I talked to her at length about Lucy having moved from an English speaking area to a Welsh speaking area, when we adopted her and the huge difficulties that this had brought about, she seemed to be remarkably interested, listening intently and she hung on every word that I said to her, she promised me that if we moved to the area she would do everything in her power to help Lucy.

I came away from the school with a hop, skip and a jump in my steps, that was indeed a huge load off my mind as Lucy's education was paramount.

The next day I felt particularly relaxed, wandering around the village, I felt just as if I was on some kind of holiday, I visited every cafe in the village, once again chatting to all of the locals, I then visited most of the shops, every person that I had a small conversation with were really friendly and kind towards me, in fact in a strange kind of way I thought that I was already living there.

I returned to see the house owner, as I always did like to deal directly with a house owner rather than trying to do a deal through an estate agent, he turned out to be a nice friendly man, offered me a cup of tea and biscuits, introduced me to his wife, we chatted for around an hour, I then made him an offer, he said, "I will tear your hand off for that" so the deal was done, I obviously had to tie up the deal through the estate agent, I then went to see a solicitor and his assistants who had done work for me many years earlier in order for him to sort out all of the legal bits, they were very pleased to see me again.

So job done, I had found a new home for us all, for now, it was back to Wales, I had a good journey, churning over in my mind all of the things that I needed to do and organise for our move to Scotland,
I knew that I had quite a few problems to sort out. It was really great to arrive home and show Hollie and Lucy pictures of our proposed new home and some literature on the village, the map came out, and we were all starting to get excited. The first thing I had to do was to sell our house in Wales, it turned out to be not a problem, it was a lovely grand old house and it sold extremely quickly.

One problem was our frozen food, Hollie always freezes any spare vegetables that we do not eat fresh from the garden and our chest freezer was full to the brim with organic vegetables, we had three choices, one, throw them away, two, give them away to neighbours or three, we could take them with us to Scotland, we decided on the latter as genuine organic vegetables are often difficult to buy anyway and those that are often sold as being organic are not, they are in fact laced with chemicals, often sold to people unscrupulously as organic.
As the removal company did not have a truck with a generator on board and as the trip for them would take at least two days to get there, all of our vegetables would have melted, another problem was that we had two cars and a motor home that had be transported up too Scotland.

Hollie didn't relish the idea of driving her car on such a long trip, I said to her, being a good husband, that I would somehow get both the cars up to our new home.

I already had a small trailer, the type with a roof, it was rather like the back section of a small van with a large opening door at the back, but would our chest freezer fit inside it? I very carefully measured the inside of the trailer could we get the freezer inside? Yes, it would just fit inside with about two centimetres either side to spare, that prompted me to ring the gentleman from whom I was purchasing the house, I asked him, "Can I please bring a freezer that will need to be plugged in and a trailer plus a car both of these will need to be parked in your driveway?

He without a moments hesitation agreed, bearing in mind at that point in time the purchase of his house had not reached completion everything hinged on a handshake.

They Probably Thought That I Had Gone Mad

From then on in, it was all systems go, I hitched up the trailer to the back of my car, Hollie then helped me, we emptied the freezer, then we put a couple of planks of wood from the ground up onto the back of the trailer then shoved the freezer bit by bit up these planks until it finally went inside the trailer, we then set about putting all of the frozen vegetables back into the freezer, covering them with lots of newspapers then we closed the lid, Phew! to a sigh of relief, we then wrapped up the outside as best as we could because of very limited space with a whole load of blankets, then off I then went to Scotland, it took me around eleven hours in total including a couple of breaks to get to our new home.

The vendors were very obliging helping me to unload my prized organic vegetables, they probably thought that I had gone mad, thankfully all of the vegetables were still frozen solid, with absolutely zero thawing out, it was then just a case of removing the freezer from the trailer moving it into the house then plugging the freezer plug into an electric socket, job well done. I then left the car and trailer at the house, the vendors wife then very kindly took me early the next morning to the nearest railway station in order for me to get local trains almost as far as Edinburgh then on to Manchester then a Virgin train back to Wales, then local trains back to my final destination.

It was all quite an experience for me as I had never before been over the Forth Bridge on a train before, this iconic bridge painted in its India red colour was a sight for sore eyes, the height I am told at its highest point is some 361 feet, the sad thing about it is that 73 men and boys lost their lives during its construction that started in 1883, it is truly a marvel of engineering skills, its a lasting testament and a tribute to all of those who lost their lives during its construction. As I travelled over the bridge the whole train and carriages seemed to roll back and forth quite a lot and I could hear the bridge groaning, I was loving every minute of it.

In fact I thoroughly enjoyed the whole journey through Edinburgh, Manchester then on down to Cardiff, one is able too see far more than when travelling by car, in fact certain parts of the journey were quite eye openers.
I noted especially when people got on the train at Edinburgh railway station, the carriage soon completely filled up with people, they all seemed to be totally obsessed and mesmerized by their laptops and mobile phones, in fact I could hardly believe my eyes and ears, they were either bellowing into their mobile phones or glued to their laptop screens, many at the same time were scoffing what looked like bacon sandwiches and shouting at their mobile phones with their mouths full of food, much of which was splattering all over the place, I thought how awful! Whatever has this world come too, it was like a mad hatters breakfast party.
A friend was waiting for me to arrive at the final railway station on my journey, I was grateful for that as the weather started to play up with high winds and heavy rain, I made it safely home.

Then I had to do the same thing all over again, this time taking Hollies car and leaving that in Scotland, thankfully with no trailer this time, so I then took exactly the same route by car up to Scotland then on various trains back to Wales. I must say that I found the second journey very much easier having done the previous journey, because I then new on my return just where to get on and off different trains at the various stations, where I had to change trains, not being at all familiar with train journeys, I did find that part of the two journeys quite daunting as very often there was no-one to ask, 'Is that my train' in fact at one stage I wondered if I had got on the wrong train, years ago when I did travel a fair bit on the trains, I remember that back then there was always railway staff on hand to help, sadly that is not the case nowadays.

That just left us with the motor home for us all to travel in, Hollie, Lucy and myself and not forgetting our three poodles and Sooty the cat to get us all up to Scotland. I was beginning to feel a bit tired from all of this travelling.
The solicitor in Scotland and the one in Wales all credit due to them handled the sale and purchase exceptionally well, we would soon be ready to go. The removal company employees came into our home to pack all of our goods and chattels, it took them around three days, then came the day

to move house, two huge trucks arrived, they had difficulty getting up the driveway because of overhanging tree branches and the power supply line to the house, however as usual removal men seem to have a knack of overcoming obstacles and taking it all in their stride they had a long pole with an insulated end on it shaped like a V, this was used to raise up the offending branches and the insulated power cables, this enabled them to drive the trucks up to the house with zero damage to their trucks or the trees and electricity cables.

They had with them a whole load of men who immediately got to work, even so it took many hours of back breaking work to load the trucks, we supplied the customary tea and biscuits, then having loaded and saying their goodbyes off they went, it was going to be a two day trek for them followed by a two day return trip. We stayed behind for a bit in order to give the house a final sweep and clean, Hollie as usual took great pride in leaving a house spick and span for the new owners.

While Hollie was giving the house a final clean, I called round to see our neighbours to say our goodbyes, the were three couples in particular who had always been very good friends ever since we first moved in, one was an artist, I used to visit him on a regular basis, he gave us a going away present of a signed pencil drawing of our house, it was superb, the next neighbour was a builder who had done lots of work on our house and finally another dear couple who always invited us round to have a cup of tea at least once a week, they were all sorry to see us go, however I had explained to them our reason for going, they all popped round to see Hollie for the final farewell.

The motorhome was full of fuel and ready to go, this was also laden with boxes full of sentimental items that we didn't want to get broken, then in jumped Lucy, then Hollie quickly followed by Winston, Emily, Sophie and Sooty, we were almost ready for the off, all of us embarking on a new future, however as with all of the dogs that we have ever had they would be happy living in a tent as long as they were with us.

We were in a way sad to go as we absolutely loved the house we were about to leave, but as we had all agreed unanimously that it was essential for Lucy's future learning and well being that we had to go.

Lucy just had to come first, so I quickly had a final look around the inside and outside of the house, just a final check to see that we had not left anything behind, I then locked the door of the house for the final time, I said in my mind a quick goodbye Wales, got back in the drivers seat started the engine and off we went heading for a new life in Scotland.

Move Number Four

We were both adamant that this little girl Lucy who had been entrusted to our care would be looked after by us to the very best of our ability, therefore for the sake of Lucy's education, it was goodbye Wales and hello Scotland, the move went like clockwork, we had a faultless journey, But, Lucy did say a few times, "Are we nearly there dad," we stopped five times for a break and something to eat and drink, then finally arriving at the village that would be our home, I was obviously a little bit concerned as Hollie and Lucy had only seen pictures of of our new home, I thought before I take them to the house I would take them on a quick spin around the village, around and around I went pointing out various plus points that I thought would please them, Lucy said that she liked the look of what would be her new school, they absolutely loved all of the little shops and were in raptures about the little harbour and the beach, I then went up to the area where we were going to live, I turned the motor home into the road were the house was situated and before I could say that's your new home they both shouted out "That's it" they had both recognised it immediately, Hollie said "Its lovely" followed by Lucy saying "I like it dad," I heaved a big sigh of relief.

They both walked in the house, in awe, being a grand old Victorian granite house, one would find it hard not to like it, we all walked around the rooms, they both commented that they liked the sizes of the downstairs rooms and they loved the big ornate open fireplaces, Hollie was in raptures about the Aga cooker, I must admit I was a little concerned about that because of its colour it was deep purple, but if Hollie liked it, it was ok by me, I had scored yet again, as they continued to explore the rest of the house with Ooohhh's and Aaaarrr's, I took the opportunity to have another good look around the garden, where I was privileged to meet our new neighbours over the garden wall, an elderly couple named Phillip and his wife Dawn, they were to become extremely good close friends.

Hollie and Lucy both told me that they absolutely loved the house and that I had made a good choice. The next day the furniture arrived from Wales, the unloading of everything went well as this time Hollie had her finger on the button, she made sure that everything went in the correct room, the removal men were very efficient that made the whole job easier when it came to the future unpacking bit. The removal men were all happy, saying that they were going to spend the night in Edinburgh on the way home as it was a place they liked but, did not get the opportunity to see the City very often, I gave them a tip so that they could get some refreshments there, they were a lovely bunch of guys.

It took a few weeks to get straight, however, it was somewhat easier than some of our previous moves as all of the rooms were livable, some of the colours of the walls were not quite to our taste but we could put up with them until we could find the time in the future to put our stamp on the house. In fact I was very pleased with the way Hollie and Lucy settled in, it was just as if we had all lived there for years and as I thought they both loved the the little local shops in the village, which were within very easy walking distance from the house.

Lucy twice a day would take the dogs for a walk along the beach, I very often joined her, it was delightful because of the stunning scenery. But, how about her new school? Lucy took to it like a duck to water and true to her word the head teacher went overboard on helping Lucy, Lucy also made a lot of new friends and Hollie an myself got to be friends with Lucy's new found friends parents.

Lucy often stayed over at her friends homes over weekends, she enjoyed that, she also enjoyed meeting another new friend who lived just one hundred metres along the same road as our new home.

I was glad that I dismantled and re-erected Lucy's big double swings and slide that we had bought for Lucy as a welcoming and birthday present in Wales, we dismantled it and erected it in the back garden of our new home in Scotland, it took a bit of work to do that, but the rewards far outweighed any effort as Lucy and all of her new found friends spent hours and hours on the swings and slide.

Hollie and Myself continued to meet lots and lots of parents of children through Lucy being friends with even more children that she met at school, also as a matter of course whenever we move house, I always go door knocking at our nearest neighbours homes to break the ice, have a little chat with them, tell them where we are from and things like that, its a great way to get to know them.

I also make a point once we get to know them, to get Lucy to visit their homes and give them a bag of organic vegetables that we have spare, people seem to like that, its amazing over the years people in return often volunteer to water my greenhouse if we go go away on holiday, others have volunteered to look after and feed Sooty, this kind of thing has happened time and time again, also they often give Lucy a little bag of sweets or a little gift, the old saying is very true' There is more happiness in giving than receiving,' there is another very big plus, we have made many, many good friends and got to know some incredibly nice people, just by being friendly with our neighbours.

Lucy used the local library from day one, she had by now become a particularly avid reader, she also continued to read the daily newspapers, we then bought Lucy a new electric organ it was free standing a bit like a piano, we were both continuing to be impressed by the progress that Lucy was making.

We booked weekly piano lessons for her, this helped her no end, she eagerly went to these lessons and was really enjoying it, our house became filled with the music from popular films soundtracks, children's songs, pop songs, and country and western songs and many more varieties of piano music, here was this little girl who in her earlier years was special needs, couldn't see properly, had been deaf for years, now really beginning to excel in all kinds of ways, it made us enormously proud of her.

Life was good, we all loved the house and garden, the previous owners just liked to have an easy mow lawned garden, so that left us with a large blank canvas, with Lucy's help we planted apple, pear and plum trees all around the walls of the garden, then I rotavated much of the lawn, even so, leaving quite a large area for Lucy and her friends to play on.
I then started to plant vegetable seeds, they had priority as we all loved to eat fresh organic garden produce, the frozen vegetables that I had brought from Wales would last us until the new crops were ready to harvest.

We Were Able To Spot Dolphins Most Days

Then came the turn of the house, we got a plumber, electrician and a builder to carry out various works, we ordered a new conservatory for the back of the house, and I painted and decorated the inside of the house from top to bottom.
Lucy was getting along fine, we were still helping her all we could.
To start with I used to walk with her to her new school and then meet her out after school, I enjoyed that, she was able to tell me of any problems she was having, or indeed any good things that she was enjoying, how she felt about things in general, how her lessons were going, I continued to do this for a few weeks, after which she walked to school with her new found friends.
On many days while Lucy was at school, Hollie and myself would take a stroll along the many paths adjacent to the beach, the scenery was mind boggling, we were able to spot dolphins most days, sometimes we were able to see them catching fish to eat, they would encircle the fish, around and around they would go in a splashing frenzy, that was quite a spectacular thing to watch.

Often on light nights or at weekends Lucy would join us and we would take the dogs along with us, Winston Emily and Sophie, always on their leads and we always made sure that we carried with us a pocket full of poo bags.

We would often see how many different kinds of birds we could spot, on other walks we would count and name if possible all of the butterflies and moths that we saw, if we didn't recognise a certain one, we would research it when we got home in our many books on the subject, other days we would do the same with, wild flowers, seashells, fish, crabs, seaweeds, different coloured stones and fossils, trees, clouds, grasses, lizards, snakes, frogs and toads and on clear nights we would just marvel at the stars in the sky, we always encouraged Lucy to really appreciate what a wonderful world that we live in.

In Scotland around June it stays light for much of the night, Hollie often had to call me in from the garden, I would be digging or something like that, absolutely oblivious to the time, she would call out "Darling do you know that it will soon be midnight" Lucy's area of garden would always look neat and tidy, however, I must say that I did lend her a hand sometimes to keep it looking good.

Hollie and myself would always attend school open days or sports days, I must confess that I do not think that Lucy will ever be chosen to represent the UK in the Olympic Games, bless her heart, she never did like sports very much, despite a lot of encouragement from us to enjoy her sporting activities. We even enrolled Lucy a local tennis club buying her all the correct gear, she went for about a year, however, her heart was not in it. We always made a point of visiting her head teacher on a fairly regular basis, to enquire on Lucy's progress, it helped to keep the teachers on their toes, I have to say that the head teaches comments regarding Lucy were always favourable.

Lucy loves book shops, boot sales, antique shops and things like that, when she first came with us she had a couple of Enid Blyton books she has since added to her collection of them, she is able to spot them in a second, she now has bookshelves full, of them, often picking up quite rare editions for a few pence, in fact she is teaching us about them. We made a point of taking her on a regular basis to theatres and live shows, she really enjoys a whole variety of entertainment from ballet, orchestral music, pop stars, country and western music, which is nice for a young girl to have such a varied taste.

On cold winter nights from the house garden we would often go outside with Lucy to watch the Northern Lights, Aurora Borealis, these spectacular light shows were just like huge mainly green swaying curtains hanging down from the sky they were absolutely breathtaking and beautiful, everyone should definitely try and at least see them once in their lifetime a real wonder to behold.

Lucy was progressing really fast enjoying life and we were also enjoying life in her company, it certainly kept us young, being mum and dad to an exceptionally lively young girl. Lucy kept in touch with her friends in Wales, mainly by letter and her homemade cards, she was now quite a proficient letter writer and she loved making things, in particular cards, made with folded card, she decorates each one with great care using pressed flowers or leaves, she likes to pick the leaves in the autumn when they are vivid reds and orange, she presses them between old book pages, or she also buys stickers of dogs, cats, flower, butterflies and all manner of different subjects, she then finds little sayings or rhymes to go inside the cards or she makes them up herself, even if I say so myself, I am astounded by the time, care, and patience that she has shown in the making of these almost professional looking beautiful cards, all credit due to her.

It is noteworthy that Lucy sends cards on a regular basis to Brenda Nice who is still working for an agency in Wales. Lucy also sends her cards to Sandra Good who has retired, she is not in good health at present.
Lucy never forgets to send little messages to her former foster carer Molly Sinclair who is now sadly in a warden controlled elderly persons care accommodation, Lucy always gets replies and updates on how they are all keeping and they always wish her well either by phone or letter, in fact in personal letters to Hollie and myself, they state that they are absolutely astounded by the way that Lucy has progressed in her life.

Lucy Then Starts Crying, Shortly Afterwards Hollie Gets Her Hankie Out And Starts To Cry

We make a point of visiting them all about every second year and my goodness aren't they over the moon to see our Lucy and they always comment on how she has grown. Molly Sinclair is now unfortunately in a wheelchair on a permanent basis, she has regular carers who call daily a couple of times to help her to wash and dress plus cook her a meal, she obviously no longer fosters children, her face really lights up and shines when we visit her, she then has a little cry, Lucy then starts crying, shortly afterwards Hollie gets her hankie out and she starts to cry, I then find it very hard to hold back the tears. Molly then tells us that we were definitely without one shadow of a doubt the right couple to adopt Lucy, with tears running down her cheeks, with a big smile on her face, bless her.

We usually then meet Sandra Good in a restaurant where we have tea and cakes together and have a good chat about how Lucy is getting along, Sandra always wants to know all of the news, as she was the main one in helping us in the adoption of Lucy, without Sandra I do not believe that it would ever have happened, so our dear friend Sandra will always have a very special place in our hearts.

Brenda Nice, is a hard lady to catch, we have planned to call on her several times, however she is always out on calls helping other couple to adopt children, we keep in constant touch by letter and hopefully in the very near future we will be able to meet Brenda and talk to her face to face, this dear Lady is also always in our thoughts, she played a huge role in helping us to adopt Lucy, we love her very dearly. Regarding Felicity Cool, we have since lost all contact with her, however, we have recently heard that she is now doing a totally different, less stressful job, we wish her well and thank her for the valued help that she gave us on our journey to adopt Lucy.

When we first had Lucy come to live with us, we were told by Felicity Cool that Lucy liked to watch soaps on the TV, well not being familiar with any of these programmes, I decided to do a little bit of personal research, I think the only one that I remembered watching a couple of times in the past was the one about country life in the villages and on the farm, would it be in Yorkshire? I do remember it being an innocent country life type of programme it very often came on during the daytime, so I started with that, well to my astonishment immediately I turned it on there was a couple of the cast a male and a female rolling around in bed together, and it didn't leave very much to the imagination, so that was definitely out.

Later I watched the one about a street, quite honestly it was awful, as soon as I switched the TV on a couple of chaps were fighting each other in the street, I persevered, would it get better I thought? It carried on with one family after another shouting or should I say bawling at each other in really loud aggressive speech, the conclusion that I came up with was that people who watch these types of programmes on a regular basis, must think in their minds that this is the way that one should behave? Or maybe they think that this is how it is? Thankfully I can truthfully say that it is not like that in our home, thank goodness.

Without being prudish or judgemental we decided that for us as a family to watch this kind of material would not be conducive to good family harmony. Children tend to emulate adults, so for Lucy to think that it was alright to shout and bawl at her mum and dad would be completely out of the question, we chatted together about this with Lucy and decided between us that if these types of programmes came on the TV we would either change channels or if there was nothing favourable on, to switch the TV off, read a book, have a chat, go for a walk, loose oneself in a hobby, in fact to do anything that we enjoyed doing.

That was years ago and we still to this day, stick to what we agreed back then, I must say looking back it was not a problem and it still isn't, if this kind of material comes on the TV following another programme. Lucy is the first one to say to Hollie or myself, 'Such and such a programme is now coming on, would you like me to change channels or switch the TV off.' We firmly believe that Lucy's life and mind has been greatly enhanced by not watching these programmes which very often contain extemely violent content, as I write Lucy is busy sitting opposite to me painting a paint by numbers picture of a westie dog sitting in a pretty garden backed by a gorgeous blue sky.

Lucy's local friends regularly called round to our house, they usually got lost in Lucy's bedroom only emerging for meals or to play in the garden on the swings and slide or to take the dogs out for a walk.
We did on occasions go for a swim in the local harbour, or should I rephrase that, I took Lucy for a swim in the harbour, Lucy like most other children did not seem to notice the cold water, however, I can clearly vouch that the North Sea, even at the height of summer in Scotland is absolutely freezing, in the sea with the water up to the height of my knees was usually enough for me, Lucy generally lasted in the water for around five minutes, she could not swim at the time, rather she splashed around, especially getting very excited at splashing dad.

We were all extremely happy at this time, Lucy was getting on particularly well at school getting excellent reports, we had lots of holidays and days out, one of the low points was that during a short period of time, all of our dear dogs died of old age, in fact our Winston the oldest, lived to be nineteen years of age, it is always a huge loss when you lose just one dog, but too lose three in the space of a few months is a tragedy, they were part of our family and were sadly missed, that huge greeting that one gets when you arrive home, and in the mornings on rising the first greeting you get is a wagging tail, in our case it was three wagging tails, they rejoiced in this way every day, they just loved to be with you, they are so affectionate, life without a dog would be very empty.

After a short while after the death of our beloved poodles, we all decided that a pet dog in the home was an absolute must, so we got a young black poodle who we named Digby and a westie who we named Sophie.

Lucy helped us to pick the dogs out of the litters, I think that she above all missed having a pet dog to take out for walks, they are masters at getting the family out of the house, they are quick to let you know when it is time for their walkies.

The garden was now getting well established with the many flowers looking an absolute picture, plus we had lots of hanging baskets making a real splash of colour, the vegetable garden was producing a bumper crop, potatoes, carrots, lettuces, spring onions, radishes you name it they were all doing well, and we had the root crops to look forward too, turnips, parsnips, carrots in fact all root crops seem to excell in Scotland, they seem to like the slightly cooler climate. I particularly noticed that there are far less garden pests in Scotland, which was obviously good news as I never have used any toxic garden chemicals or sprays on the garden, after all, these chemicals are designed to kill, so it is very obvious that they cannot do us any good when sprayed on the food that we eat.

Lucy still enjoyed helping in the garden and Hollie lends me a hand sometimes, as time allows, however, I think that she was more in her element when cooking the vegetables rather than growing them, she always has been a master at cooking, making a lovely tasty meal out of a few humble ingredients.

Hollie and me have in fact been vegetarians for around twenty five years, Lucy when she first came with us was not. Hollie cooked her meals separately as she liked all kinds of meat, chicken, bacon and pork sausages, in fact chicken nuggets were her favourite thing to eat, I always did think that they were ghastly things, however, after Lucy had been with us for about eighteen months, we were sitting at the dinner table one evening and all of sudden completely her own decision right out of the blue she asked to eat in future the same meals as we ate. We are not strictly vegetarian as we also eat fish, eggs and cheese, nevertheless, Lucy by her own decision from that moment on saved Hollie an awful lot of extra work in the kitchen and I must say, as they say in Scotland, Lucy looked a Bonnie Wee Lass on her new diet made up in the main by organic home grown vegetables.

Life Was Good

Another thing that we consider important that we do is that we always sit down together with Lucy, for our breakfast, lunch and dinner at the dining table, it is not only more comfortable and relaxing but we have also found that it a great time to talk to each other about our day and what we are planning to do tomorrow, we even discuss future holidays or what shows we are planning to visit and things like that, its also a good relaxing time to sort out any little problems that we might have, Lucy normally highlights what happened at her school, or sometimes we just have a good laugh at the various things that we have done, seen or read that day.

Life was good, in fact I would go so far as to say that it was very good. Lucy was fast approaching the age where she would have to change schools, could anything possibly affect what was now a remarkably good period in all of our lives?

An official looking letter arrived through our letter box, it was from the Local Planning Office, the letter stated that a mobile phone operator had submitted plans to erect a new 3rd Generation Electromagnetic Radiation Mobile Phone Mast just a few metre's away from our home, although I wasn't very pleased, I didn't at the time give it a second thought at first, then after a while I started to do a little research into this technology.

I was horrified straight away as I found out that Mobile Phone Technology uses the same frequency as used in domestic and commercial microwave ovens, microwave ovens operate at 915 MHz and 2450 MHz.. (2.45 Ghz) Mobile Phones 3rd Generation operate at 2200 MHz..(2.2GHz)

So 3rd Generation Electromagnetic Radiation Mobile Phone technology operates at the same frequency and very often higher than microwave ovens that people use in their kitchens to cook their meals or heat up their food or drinks, we all know what happens if you put a bowl of water in a microwave oven, it very quickly boils, you are probably also very well aware that a very large proportion of the human body and brain are made up of water, you can no doubt see where I am coming from.

'Precautionary Approach'

Although we are told that the power of the mobile phone signal is not usually enough to cause heating? Unless of course the mobile phone mast is malfunctioning in some way or another or National Guidelines are not correct? Very importantly there are also non- thermal influences in these emissions from Mobile Phone Masts or Base Stations as mobile operators like to call them known as (The Non Thermal Effect) this non-thermal effect appears to show a greater need to depend on the frequency rather than the heating effect of the electromagnetic radiation emissions.

Mobile Phone emissions were showing, judging by news reports ever more signs of causing unfavourable health reactions to ever greater numbers of people, especially those who were being exposed too twenty four hour a day, three hundred and sixty five days a year electromagnetic radiation from these mobile mast emissions.

There were numerous reports of people living near these Mobile Phone Masts reporting suffering all kinds of health problems, including cancer clusters, a mast was reportedly being moved to an alternative site due to the death of a little girl.

This prompted me to look further into the potential dangers from this technology, I needed to know if our Lucy was at risk, not only Lucy but all other children, every child has a human right to be kept safe.

Over the last few years *gradualism has crept in,* because we were being told that this technology was safe, however, the people who are telling us this, as you will see as you read on that most of them appear to have absolutely not got a clue what is happening, they even tell us that they do not understand why certain things are happening in the human brain as a result of peoples exposure to electromagnetic microwave radiation.

I wanted to find out more, because of the proposed erection of this 2nd Generation Electromagnetic Radiation Mobile Phone Mast right near to our home, which they informed me would be changed to 3rd generation after a period of three years, I started by writing letters to The Mobile Phone Company who were proposing to erect this mast, Their agents, The UK Government, The Local Authority, The National Radiological Protection Board, which changed its name to The Health Protection Agency, it has now unbelievably changed its name yet again to Public Health England, (Surely all of these name changes tells us that something is not quite right) Members Of The European Parliament, various Members of the UK Parliament, The Scottish Executive/Government and many more people who had an interest in this technology, in fact I sent letters to any group, company or persons whom I thought could stop this mast being erected.

It turned out to be enormously helpful as scores of reply letters, leaflets and informative information was sent to me from these various, diverse organizations and people, it just poured through my letter box.

The information that I received from of these people all connected in some way or other to mobile technology or from those people having concerns about it or indeed people who could possibly stop it from being erected. That is where my knowledge was gleaned from, the very people who should have all the answers,? what did concern me was that many of these people or organizations outlined loads of health dangers, many they admitted or reported were already said to be rampant amongst people having to live near mobile phone masts.

This puzzled me, as much of the information from these people stated in a whole load of other vague information, disputing that their were dangers to health. I then thought to myself, that's strange they cannot have it both ways, either it is harmful to human health or it isn't, so I set about trying to find the real truth by delving into this huge pile of information that I had been sent

There were many warnings that there were indeed health problems connected with this Mobile Technology, and as a result of people living near these mobile masts, reports like loss of memory, vertigo, loss of concentration, irregular heartbeat, (Which may well be the reason for the enormous rise in strokes and heart attacks in much younger people in the last few years) chronic headaches, skin problems, nausea, dizziness, fatigue, shortness of breath, abnormal sweating even that cancer clusters were being reported around these mobile masts, there were also warnings of biological effects taking place at below national safety guidelines.

In addition it was highlighted that Mobile Phone Emissions were causing electromagnetic hypersensitivity for a huge number of people, time and time again there were warnings about taking a (Precautionary Approach) regarding this technology was very important.

Further to this it was highlighted in this information, that changes in brain activity can happen at below national safety guidelines and they do not know why?

In Sweden it was reported that people who have used a mobile phone for ten years or more are suffering increases in acoustic neuromas which are benign tumours that grow on the nerve that links the ear to the brain, if they continue to grow in size they can cause facial paralysis, they have been known to grow large and press on peoples brains, if they reach this stage they can threaten ones life.

Other written reports clearly state that electromagnetic fields were causing people to suffer from Depression, Childhood Leukaemia, Cataracts, Tinnitus, Brain Tumours and Alzheimer's caused it is thought by peoples immune systems are being impaired, some of the forgoing are said by experts in this field to be caused by very low doses of non- ionising radiation.

I started to think that the bulk of these problems as mentioned in the information and reply letters sent to me were nearly all connected with the human brain like, loss of memory, vertigo, loss of concentration, dizziness, anxiety, chronic headaches, these were the ones listed, as being reported by the people who are supposed to protect our health. Then there are far more serious things affecting the human brain like Alzheimer's, Parkinson's and Super Nuclear Palsy, which are now becoming a huge scourge throughout the whole world, could they now be a follow on? A possible connection surely cannot be dismissed.

I understand that tests regarding this technology are in the main short term immediate effects carried out on bits of dead animal meat/tissue and very few tests have been carried out on live human beings, That beggars belief! Perhaps they consider it to dangerous to carry out tests on human beings? A dead bit of animal flesh cannot possibly give a meaningful reaction, as it is non- functioning. Non-thermal tests would only be a worthwhile and purposeful exercise on something alive, and not dead, as something dead will have totally zero discernable electrical brain function. I am not encouraging tests on live animals as I think that any live animals should not be experimented upon under any circumstances.
If human beings volunteer to such barmy tests it is obviously up to them.

Mobile Phone Operators told me that they set their operating standards to guidelines as laid down by International Standards, judging by the foregoing which are gleaned from the replies that I received from the various organizations and overseers of our health protection from this technology in the UK, it would seem to me that these guidelines are not up to scratch, if health problems are occurring at below these International Safety Guidelines and Standards and a (Precautionary Approach) is required, it is basic common sense that these guidelines very urgently need to be changed and safety standards improved to protect human health.

The strength of the signal in the UK is stated to be the highest in the world, it is in fact said to be three million times higher than considered to be safe levels in Australia.
(Its interesting that bees are thriving in Australia they even have a huge export market for them sending them all over the world, See Later)

It is worthy of note that many countries in Europe have adopted a signal strength far lower than those recommended by the ICNIRP.

The information and letters that I received from these various people and organizations prompted me to take closer look in depth at all of this information. For instance I was informed that the balance of evidence shows that there was supposed to be *'No General Risk To Health'* from Mobile Phone Technology. Just what were they trying to tell us members of the public. Firstly, if there are 'NO' risks to human health why not say so in plain English? *'No Risk To Health'* there we are, everybody would understand that.

No General Risks To Health is an extremely vague terminology as the word 'General' means according to my dictionary; (Indefinite, Broad, Sweeping, Vague, rough, Ill-Defined, Inexact, Imprecise) it sounds very woolly, nebulous and totally unclear to me.

They then highlight that there is evidence of changes in brain activity and they have not got a clue why? They also state that biological effects are occurring at below the current safety standards that this mobile technology operates by.

Its No Wonder Many People Are Concerned

Warning were then given to say that young children should refrain from using a mobile phone, they then go on to say that it is not possible to say if it will affect peoples health because of gaps in their knowledge and the technology is surging ahead at a faster rate than they can analyse it for health problems. It is no wonder many people are concerned.

On top of all the aforementioned health problems they then tell us that we all need to take a (Precautionary Approach) towards this technology. Isn't it pretty logical that if as they state, this mobile technology was not dangerous to human health? Why! Oh! Why! Would we need to be told to take a (Precautionary Approach.)

The very latest advice from them, sent to me as recently as Oct. 2013 is for a (Precautionary Approach) this is recommended to be continued, because they again state that the use of handsets (Mobile Phones) should be limited because of exposures owing to the devices proximity to the human head when calls are being made, (That seems a pretty logical statement, what else would you do with a phone?) They then tell us as exposures are much higher from a mobile phone than those from a base station, (Mobile Phone Masts) it is also recommended that mobile phone use by children should be limited (Kept Short) and for young people under 16 should be encouraged to use a mobile phone for essential purposes only. Ask yourself why? If they are not a danger to our children.

It then crazily stated, that they will monitor the emerging scientific evidence, provide any necessary advice and undertake another comprehensive review of the science once sufficient evidence has accumulated. (That all sounds a bit late to me)

Call me cynical, but how can they possibly say that there is 'No General Risk To Health,' after outlining a whole host of health problems already being reported as caused by the technology, stating that there are many things happening within peoples brains, changes in brain activity and they do not know why?

Also that they cannot keep up with the analysing of health problems that the technology may well be causing because of the speed that the technology is surging forward, just by saying that they cannot keep up with the analysing of any future the health problems because of the speed that this technology is advancing is crazy, surely one would want to find out if it was harmful to human health before unleashing it on the public.

On reading all of this stuff, to any thinking person it is absolute balderdash vague, uncertain, unsettled, unresolved, haphazard and downright nonsensical, just lots of weazel words and jargon and vague excuses, because from what I was reading it was pretty obvious that they do not fully understand or have a clue themselves, just what damage this technology can inflict on the human race, making us all guinea pigs,
Rest assured if it was safe they would be the very first ones to tell us.

It is very important to note at this point that TV and radio mast emissions are NOT PULSED in any way that can be recognised by the human brain. Some mobile mast operators erroneously make a strong habit of comparing the potentially harmful pulsed microwave emissions from their mobile phone masts/ base stations to Radio and TV mast emissions, is it possible that they say this, in order to be able to say that we have lived with these Radio and TV mast emissions for years with no harm to human health?

By this flawed stratagem comparison method that they were sounding out, could it possibly be that they are trying to confuse and mollify the public into thinking that mobile phone technology that they are using is safe.

To confirm this very important point a well known leading mobile phone operator, company manager in a letter that I had forwarded to me, in the letter he related to TV mast emissions comparing them to mobile phone mast emissions, stating that a TV transmitter typically runs at 100,000 (One hundred thousand watts) and a typical mobile phone mast at a mere 150 (One hundred and fifty watts), however, this comparison is way out of order and is simply not a true analogy, there is absolutely no relationship between the two, I will tell you why.

Mobile phone mast emissions are pulsed at rates that the human brain can easily identify, these pulsed microwaves penetrate directly through the human skull and into the human brain, radio waves are not the problem, but rather its the way that mobile phone technology uses them, mobile phone emissions are pulsed in short, repetitive, recurrent, bursts transmitted on a microwave frequency this seems to be very much more detrimental to us humans.

Radio and TV mast emissions are Not Pulsed and are a steady lower frequency signal therefore they are not recognised by the human brain.

It was emphasised in the information that I had received that they were aware that the frequency of the radiation from these mobile phone masts seems to interfere with the human bodies own electrical /lectrochemical rhythms. Many scientists are now saying that the only safe dose of man-made pulsed radiation is zero.

From what I was learning, I was obviously concerned by the health implications and how they could affect our Lucy all other children and indeed ourselves, I could stop Lucy from having or using a mobile phone, even so, once this mobile phone mast was erected and in operation very close to our home, I would have zero control over the electromagnetic radiation frequency emissions coming from the mast twenty four hours a day, seven days a week, for years. This quite obviously must be potentially extremely dangerous to humans, despite mobile phone operators saying that they are not a danger to health but they say, there may be *limited harm* whatever they mean by that? What limited harm? Just how harmful is this limited harm going to be? Surely if it was NOT harmful to humans they would have stated, Harmless, once again its weasel words.

Bearing in mind that each exposure that we all have to radiation, however extremely tiny the dose it builds up in our bodies, each and every time we are exposed to it, our bodies are constantly during the day and especially night in a repair mode to rectify any damage done to our body, but now with this constant bombardment of round the clock electromagnetic microwave radiation enhanced greatly by Mobile Phone Masts and Mobile Phones, all adding to the dangers of electromagnetic smog that surrounds us all, is it possible our bodies now starting to be overwhelmed by it all? As those people living near these masts despite the electromagnetic microwave radiation emissions being low? It is a constant day and night exposure, thus never giving their bodies the chance to heal the damage being done, however limited that might be?

In many countries there are laws that prohibit the erection of these masts close to where people live, many state that they must be at least five hundred (500) metres away from peoples homes, wouldn't it be wise to have similar laws in the UK. In fact it probably would be wise to put them even greater distances away from where people live.

Many products in the past have proved to be harmful to human health, Procrastination by those who had the power to deal with these things caused many unnecessary deaths and much suffering was caused by the use of products like Asbestos, DDT, Cigarettes and lead in Petrol and Paint. We only have to think of the death of our dear friend Tom , caused by the use of one of these highly dangerous toxic products.

One might choose to use a mobile phone only a few times a day or for emergency use only, however people who live near a mobile phone mast do not have the luxury of choice, in fact they have no choice at all, other than to be bombarded by electromagnetic radiation 24 hours a day 365 days a year, brick walls and closing ones doors or windows is no defence against this technology. Hence all of the reports from people living near these masts of health problems.

Parents take note, I then discovered that because children's internal organs are not fully developed, therefore, this unnatural electromagnetic microwave pulsed radiation can interfere with a young child's develop- ment as it is well known microwaves can cause significant damage to the DNA of living cells even at extremely low doses making this technology potentially much more dangerous to a young child or indeed an unborn child.

Hollie and myself were obviously concerned about this technology and the affect it may well have on our Lucy's health and not just Lucy but also for all of the children who regularly play in a children's play area very close to where this proposed mast was going to be erected and indeed to any child or grown up person anywhere in the world.

This prompted me to look at this technology in even greater depth, my research clearly showed that it was not just the mobile phone masts but also the mobile phones themselves and you cannot have one without the other, warnings about this technology highlighted that the risks to children were a real concern, alarmingly the messages warned that the younger the child, the greater risk was to that child, however, it is now reported that parents in the UK are giving mobile phones to their children aged five and under, it is estimated that over one million children under five years old now have a mobile phone, and one in three children now have a mobile phone *before they can talk.*

In one of many letters sent to me by a Mobile Phone Operator Manager. This statement stood out;
'Insofar as some limited harm may be perceived this is outweighed by modern communications.'
The writer gave no clear answer to what limited harm that he thought might be inflicted upon us humans, however what is patently clear was that whatever harm we or our children might have to suffer, it appears that to him, that it was not as important as this modern mobile technology. Nowhere in his letter was there any reference to the thought of his Mobile Phone Company taking a (Precautionary Approach.)

From a member of the Scottish Executive/ Government, I got this reply letter.
I would agree that the situation with regard to the erection of a mobile phone mast is very frustrating with the phone companies holding most of the cards. The Scottish Executive (Government) have shown themselves loath in the extreme from getting involved in the health argument, preferring instead to issue vague answers in the hope that the issue will go away.
Yours Sincerely

It appears from the information that I had received that the area of highest potential danger from Mobile Phone Masts, which was our main concern at that time, is that maximum fields from mobile phone masts at ground level occurs between 30 metres and 100 metres from the mast/ base station, it can then continue for a radius of 10 kilometres or even more, however even at these distances latest reports clearly highlight that biological effects to the human body can still occur.

In a Town or City its signals radius may be only be around a few score metres, then the next masts signal overlaps with that masts signal and so it goes on to cover the whole Town or City.
In the case of our house, we were well within this potentially most dangerous too health area, when I pointed this out to the Mobile Phone Operator Executive concerned with the proposed erection of this mast, his reply was;
"You are lucky if you lived in a City you would probably find a Mobile Phone Mast every 50 metres.

I then asked myself where are all of these tens of thousands of Mobile Masts? I had absolutely no idea that there was this huge amount of Mobile Phone Masts in a Town or City, I felt that I just had to find out?
They are in fact being hidden, its no wonder that most of them were not visible to the public.
I found out that Local Authority Planning Departments have thick glossy brochures full of drawn pictures and photographs that make suggestions on how to cunningly, secretly hide these masts from the public, they show how to hide them in petrol signs, shop signs, road signs in fake chimneys, they are even incorporated in public works of art, some are disguised as street lamps, many are hidden in church spires, there is even one shown to be incorporated in an angel weathervane on the top of a cathedral spire, still others are hidden in fake trees.

This is pretty serious stuff because, do you think that they are seriously considering a (Precautionary Approach) by allowing and giving approval and encouragement for the erection of these tens of thousands of secretly hidden from sight Mobile Phone Masts.
It was fairly obvious that Planning Departments were working very closely along with the Mobile Phone Operators as this is highlighted in the advice given by them to the operators.
I would personally say that this is a potentially extremely dangerous tactic because of the warnings given out, that there are significant gaps in mankind's knowledge of this technology, and they will continue to monitor the emerging scientific evidence and undertake another comprehensive review of the science once sufficient evidence has accumulated.
Their words not mine, is that not absolutely daft, surely any sane person would make sure that the evidence was monitored before potentially putting every single person living in the UK, health at risk.

It was very easy to see why Local Authority Planning Departments actively encourage the secret concealing and disguising of Mobile Phone Masts, because there were thousands and thousands of people protesting that they didn't want these Electromagnetic Radiation Horrors near to their homes and rightly so.
However, this scatterbrained, ill thought out and totally irresponsible, negligent plan to secretly camouflage, thus, hide these masts from the publics view, very obviously makes them acutely very much more dangerous for families with young children who are according to the experts at potentially a much greater risk from this technology.

As these people cannot see these masts, therefore there is absolutely no way that these families could possibly take a (Precautionary Approach) as highly recommended by reliable reports from the worlds leading experts regarding this Mobile Technology. With many now highlighting that the mobile phone masts are potentially equally as dangerous as the phones because of the continuous radiation, be it at very low doses, because it never stops, the people near these masts have no alternative and do not have any choice, other than to be continually irradiated by the emissions from these mobile phone masts day and night.

A family or people with young children might for instance buy or rent a house, within the 30 to 100 metre danger area of these masts without ever knowing that these potentially extremely dangerous hidden secret masts are even there. Extraordinarily, I am informed that Mobile Phone Masts under 15 metres in height do not need planning permission at all, rather mast operators get away with it by using a scheme called prior notification.

With all of the goings on with the mast we thought that we would get away from it all and go on a really good holiday, we decided on the Lot region of France, we would start by taking the overnight ferry from Edinburgh Rosyth to Zeebrugge.

The departure day arrived we drove the car to Rosyth Lucy on spotting the giant ferry ship, immediately said to us, "I am not getting on that" Nevertheless after a bit of coaxing and after driving on board, she was in her element, her huge bright blue eyes really opened up as she was taking it all in.

We first of all started to have a good look around the ferry, Lucy was amazed at the sheer size of the ferry, having looked at our sleeping quarters, we then investigated the rest of the inside, then we went out on deck to have a look there, all around the lifeboats and there was some cats and dogs in an area for pets, Lucy made a fuss of one of the dogs.

Lost In France

It was then time to set sail, on leaving Rosyth the ferry headed out under the famous Forth Bridge, Lucy waved to the workmen who were working on the bridge, she was loving it despite the odd small splash of water and her getting a bit wet, her little face lit up and radiated with delight. After another wander around the ferry we then all sat down in the restaurant to the most scrumptious dinner, Lucy went back for second helpings and then off to bed.

After an all night journey down the North Sea, I did look out for Norfolk as that is where I was born, I could see quite clearly the lights of the little towns dotted along the coast, we then in the morning safely arrived in Zeebrugge, from there we motored South into France then on down planning to bypass Paris, not knowing where we were, having intended to avoid the place, by my meticulous planning for the journey we ended up slap bang in the middle of Paris during rush hour on a Friday evening as people were leaving off work, I then stopped and asked a young French boy for directions, he described in broken English the way to go, as I started to go he tapped on the car roof, I stopped and he stuck in my hand a map of Paris, Bless him.

What a hair raising place to drive, motorbikes hundreds of them were overtaking us a breakneck speeds on both sides of the car, still lost I turned off into a roadside hotel car park an unbelievably charming and helpful French lady was most kind she gave me a carefully hand drawn plan showing me the way to go, in fact by more luck than judgement we were exactly on the road that we needed to be on.
Lucy was loving all of the noise and excitement, I thought that she might possibly be alarmed by it all, not a bit of it.

After many more hours heading South we stopped at a roadside Bed and Breakfast in a small town, Hollie was tired and went straight to bed. Lucy, however, had other ideas she said to me that she was hungry, so we set out on foot to try and find somewhere to eat, we soon found a fascinating place it was a cross between a village hall, pub or club. it was absolutely packed with people of all age groups, they appeared to be in family groups mostly sitting at tables enjoying a night out, there was nobody drunk or rowdy, it was just all good family fun, there was a rock band followed by a sort of country and western style group, everyone was either drinking, eating or dancing between the tables, it was a delight. We couldn't find a soul who could speak English, so ordering some food was fun, being vegetarians it was proving difficult to get the people serving the food to understand.

I kept waving my hands and saying "No Moo! several times, getting blank looks, suddenly one of the waitresses walked past with a vegetable topped pizza in her hand, I pointed to that, then put my thumb up and nodded, that worked, within a few minutes our pizza's arrived, they were delicious, we joined in as best as we could in the sing song, it was great, poor Hollie missed all of the fun.
The next morning we were once again on our way, we were now about seventy miles from our destination, the scenery was lovely, we must have been in brown cow country as the fields were full of these healthy looking

brown cows. The holiday was a complete success, our holiday cottage was situated on a small farm right in the heart of the countryside, having English owners, they made us very welcome, often we sat with them outside in the evenings having a glass of local wine, they showed us where to collect some drinking water it came in a little waterfall straight out of the side of a huge rock overhang, it tasted superb.

On a trip out we once again got lost up in the hills in a small village, the village was not even showing on our map, we stopped, and I asked a man the way to go, he was selling vegetables, flowers and milk from a van, I tried to explain to him where we would like to head for, he threw his hands up in the air gesturing, he didn't have a clue what I was saying and likewise I couldn't understand what he was saying, up came a young man he spoke a little broken English, however he also didn't understand what we were saying, during this time up came a whole host of villages mainly ladies, they were all joining in chatting away, pointing and laughing, yet still more arrived, mainly to buy vegetables and other things, they all got involved in trying to work out where we wanted to head for, to think all of these dear people cared about us, we were all very impressed, between them they managed to worked out which way we should go, the highlight was yet to come.

We thanked everybody for their help shaking hands with them all, we then got in the car ready to go, everybody was laughing out loud really enjoying the experience, the grocery van man then opened our car door on the passenger side and gave Hollie a huge bunch of mixed flowers, what a wonderful gesture, I could see a tear in the corner of Hollie's eye, what gracious wonderful people, we will never forget that delightful holiday.

Lucy loved France, it was such an educational experience for us all especially Lucy, meeting friendly people, travelling through glorious landscapes, experiencing the delights of many restaurants, buying wine to take home straight from the many vineyards, visiting lots of local village French markets that had cheeses to die for, experiencing all of the little shops in town centres, selling everything one could possible wish to buy, Lucy bought many different items that one could not buy back in Scotland. Just looking in the rivers was an exhilarating experience with huge fish swimming around they could very clearly be seen in the unbelievably clear water.
Lucy also on this trip asked to visit and go in old churches, castles and other large old buildings, this was good because in past times on taking Lucy in cathedrals, churches and suchlike places in the UK, she would

always get tense and scared, wanting to get out of the buildings as quickly as possible, however, in France these kinds of buildings seemed to fascinate her, I didn't mind this at all as I have always loved history and historical buildings, even so, as with all things they have to come to a end, I do not think that any of us will ever forget this fabulous holiday, the introducing our little girl Lucy to this lovely country of France, it was then back home to Scotland.

To bring you up to date with the very latest 4g mobile phone technology it is said to operates at 800 MHZ and it is to be used to cover long distances and please note I am told that the emissions are not impeded by any obstacles namely hills, trees or buildings, also there is a 2.6 Ghz version this I am advised is that this version can carry more data and is said to be ideal for use in City centres, all of this sounds potentially terribly risky for human health, the fact that this very latest 4g pulsed electromagnetic radiation technology that uses more bandwidth will not be in any way be hindered, blocked or obstructed by trees, hills or buildings and according to the latest information that I recently received regarding Public Health England, is that they <u>expect</u> and *therefore trust* that it will be within international safety guidelines as it is stated to be very similar to the current mobile communications networks operating at present?

The Mobile Phone Companies Hold Most Of The Cards

That being the case, as this organization that came up with these International safety guidelines that do not appear to be up to scratch and not working, judging by the health problems of tens of thousands of people, having been highlighted as a result of the 2g and current 3g systems, as this new 4g system is said to be *similar?* to these and its electromagnetic microwave radiation emissions are not impeded in any way, which they were under the older 2g and 3g technology. It is therefore quite obviously very likely to be even more potentially dangerous to human health and especially to our young children it has been highlighted that children are potentially more at risk than grownups to the effects from this Electromagnetic Microwave Radiation technology.

I wonder what the mobile operators will say about the perceived dangers and limited harm and a (Precautionary Approach) that we should take when this 4g really gets going nationwide, it will be no good any of us trying to escape the effects of this electromagnetic radiation with its non thermal effects as it will reach every square millimetre of land throughout the UK, it will certainly be on no use relying on the bricks and mortar of our home offering any protection, this technology knows no boundary, unless of course you happen to surround yourself with a Faraday cage or have your walls lined with lead.

It is now high time to stop any further expansion of this technology until such times as the final results of the scientific accumulation of evidence they say that they are waiting for is obtained, in the meantime a very much safer method of communication needs to be urgently devised.

'We are all in this together,' that will certainly be true in this case, nobody can escape from this technology, it is now affecting all of mankind, Mobile Phone Executives, rich and poor people, in fact all of us on the planet are now living in the sea and smog of artificial frequencies, the result of it could well mean potential disaster for not just us humans, but its effects will likely threaten all insect, plants, birds and animals on this planet.

The Mobile Operator Won

In our case the mobile operator appealed against the Local Authority majority decision to stop the mast being erected near our home and won, as they did for scores of others in our area, so much for local democracy. We had absolutely no right of appeal unless of course we took the mobile phone operator to court at a huge financial cost according to the Solicitor who advised us, even if we did that, our chances of success was put at zero.

As the Scottish Parliament Member said; The mobile phone companies hold most of the cards.' I now strongly think that he was wrong, without one shadow of doubt in my opinion, they hold every one of the cards.

A very sensible bit of advice for everyone is to please read slowly and carefully the mobile phone manufacturers paper instructions and warnings contained in the small print that comes with a new mobile phone, or dig out the one you might have stuck in a drawer with a guarantee and take note of what that says, read it carefully right through to the end as the health warning bits are not usually mentioned until you are fed up with reading it, they are tucked in nearer towards the end.

Many experts warn that one should keep a mobile phone at least 15 to 25 millimetres away from your body when turned on near the head also to keep the phone these same distances from the abdomen of a woman who is pregnant the same applies to a young male person to keep a switched on mobile phone away from their lower abdomen, in fact many mobile phone manufacturers agree with much of this stating in the small print on their instruction leaflets that come with a new mobile phone, that the phones when switched on should always be kept at least 15mm from your body and at least one manufacturer states to keep the phone away from your body by 25mm (One Inch) and to reduce your time spent on the phone when it is turned on. And please specifically note that with many new style mobile phones which are now very thin, so when held directly next to the head, it is not possible to leave a distance of 25 mm (One Inch) from the phones antenna as recommended in some of the phone manufacturers small print.

Another source advises that children under eight years of age should not use a mobile phone at all. Many experts also strongly advise avoiding if possible using a mobile phone on a train or in a car, in fact try not to use it in any enclosed spaces as this will potentially be more harmful to human health, its recommended from at least one source to never use a phone for any longer than around 5 to 7 minutes at a time because radiation is absorbed through the human skull and into the brain.

Up to this point I have not mentioned mobile phones SAR ratings that means The Specific Absorption Rate, mobile phones emit radio frequency electromagnetic fields, this radiation is absorbed by the human body, the level of a persons exposure to this radiation is called the specific absorption rate, without getting to complicated what this means is that some mobile phones that you are able to purchase have a higher SAR level rating than others or the more radiation that phone emits that is absorbed by the users body, usually by the persons skull and brain, it is therefore probably a very sensible thing to do, to only purchase a mobile phone with a lower SAR level, if you must have one.

I personally never use a mobile phone, I do not own one and do not want one, I either use a land line or better still speak to people face to face, which just has to be by far, a better way to communicate with people.

Also people using these phones are now monitored as to their whereabouts and who they are in touch with, they might be called smart phones, however I cannot see anything smart in anyone's movements being tracked all day.

I will not say anything about the dangers to our young people from porn, except to say that its availability to them with just a click is deplorable.

I am informed that recent research on cancer has classified mobile phone emissions as a Group 2B Carcinogen.

My being a keen gardener for many years, many of my gardening friends and I, have noticed particularly over the last twenty or so years that many plants, insects and birds are suffering greatly, are they like us humans possibly being affected by this pulsed electromagnetic radiation and its non- thermal effects? As mobile phone mast emissions even at considerable distances away are many, many *billions of times* greater than the microwave radiation that is coming from the sun in the sky at the same frequency.

Visiting a raspberry farmer recently he expressed his great concern at a total lack of bees in the year 2012, he stated that he had seen the very odd bumble bee that's all. The same thing was very evident in my flower garden in which I have planted every possible attraction for bees, I make a really determined point of planting scores of plants that should normally attract bees, but alas in the garden the bee numbers have recently gone drastically down in number, the danger is of course, No Bee's! No Food for us humans to eat.

This phenomenon is sadly happening almost everywhere worldwide, especially in some areas of China, where farmers are having too pollinate tens of thousands of fruit trees by hand with the use of little paint brushes, many thousands of people now have to climb up ladders to pollinate the flowers, adding a huge costs to the fruit when it is eventually sold at the markets, it is patently obvious that more research urgently needs to be done, instead of these obviously very clever people in research into electromagnetic microwave radiation and its non- thermal effects saying they do not know why it is having various effects on humans, procrastination and denial could easily eventually wreak havoc on all living things.

In the UK and Europe, trees are currently beginning to suffer all manner of problems all in a very short space of time in history, ash, horse chestnut, oak and elms are all being weakened, is this mobile technology making them susceptible to these problems?

They seem all of a sudden to have have little or no resistance too various diseases and insect attacks, could it possibly be be that electromagnetic microwave radiation is the cause of these devastating problems as all of us humans all around the earth and every other living thing are now having to live in an ever increasing smog of artificial frequencies, we have to ask is this technology reaping havoc on all living things?

The so-called experts regarding this technology and the very people who are supposed to be the public's health protectors, all they can say is that they will, *'Monitor the emerging scientific evidence as it emerges and undertake a review of the science when they think that sufficient evidence has accumulated.'* Have you ever read such unscientific drivel and nonsense in all your life?

I just wonder how many more young children at Christmas had a new mobile phone given to them as a present, do you seriously think that they read every detail on the instructions and warnings that came on a piece of paper with that phone, and alarmingly parents are giving their children these phones before they can even read and those who can read are probably just reading how to switch the thing on then immediately stick it up to their ear.

There is certainly an urgent case for these mobile phones to have a danger warning etched on the plastic casing, stating the dangers of these phones, just like the warnings on the outside of cigarette packets.

It is a well known fact that moving electric fields particularly from electric power lines and now in addition pulsed electromagnetic radiation with its non thermal effects from this mobile phone technology are a potential current and present danger to humans causing all manner of health problems by impairing our bodily immune functions, so are we now nearing the tipping point, along with all other living things on this planet earth, suffering from the effects of this technology?

Why blame this technology? And not other man made pollutants?

The answer is very simple, the health problems highlighted are happening to people in every country on earth. There are now many thousands of accounts recorded of ill individual people living near mobile masts, suffering from the various health effects previously mentioned, who get better as soon as they move away from the pulsed microwave radiation from these mobile phone masts.

As this technology produces I am informed the only known man made pollution that reaches every last square millimetre of the surface of the earth and everything that is on the earths surface, it certainly seems to be the prime candidate for causing all of the earth wide problems mentioned. Only time will tell, that is of course, if we have the time?

An Eminent Professor who knows more about this technology than I ever will, said; 'I do not really think that any of us can put our hands on our hearts and say that this Mobile Phone Technology is safe.'

A final few words on this subject, always remember, people who highlight the potential dangers from this mobile technology especially from its non-thermal effects are often ridiculed and held in derision by people who are involved in the promotion of this mobile technology.

They themselves highlight that it is impossible to say that exposure to the radiation from this technology even at levels below national guidelines are not without potential, unfavourable or harmful health effects and they continue to say from information sent to me; As there is now scientific evidence suggesting that there may be biological effects occurring at exposures that are below safety guidelines and that there are gaps in their knowledge and they have absolutely no way of analysing the potential impact on human health due to the speed at which this technology is developing, (In other words they cannot keep up with it,) it is sufficient to warrant a Precautionary Approach.

And those very latest comments from them is this; *They will continue to monitor the emerging scientific evidence, provide any necessary advice and then undertake another comprehensive review of the science once sufficient evidence has accumulated? Don't Hold Your Breath!*

Therefore I would say that it is these people who need to be the objects of ridicule for trying very hard to tell us there are no dangers, after they have highlighted harmful effects already happening, they will look at it after the horse has bolted and the damage has been done, they strongly appear in my opinion to be using weasel words in order to cover over their ignorance of this technology as they do not appear to have a clue themselves.

We Decided To Move

Many of our neighbours decided to move house because of the mast, we also decided that Lucy's long term health was far more important than a house and home, so we also decided to up sticks and move.

Knowing that this mast was going to be erected in a couple of months time, gave us the time to look around for another house to live in, where should we go?

We had discussed various areas for several months, in fact since we first started our campaign to try and stop the mast being erected, we all decided that we would like to stay in Scotland, so our search began, we found two properties that we liked, the first one was a good sized bungalow in a pretty village, it had a little stream of water at the bottom of the rear garden, we all liked it, so we went back for a second viewing and we all then agreed that would be a nice home for us all, however, this time however I had a closer look at the rear garden, it had a large lawn area, that would make a super vegetable plot, as I was viewing this area, I thought to myself whatever is that smell, on a closer examination there was scattered all over the grassed area, thousands of teeny bits of toilet paper, it turned out that the owners had problems with the septic tank and it had been overflowing making the lawn into a very smelly boggy mess, that put us off the purchase of the bungalow, there is no way that I could grow my vegetables there.

We then found a fine looking house on an elevated site with distant breathtaking views of mountains, the house was within walking distance of a good school for Lucy, after us all agreeing that we would like to live there, I immediately contacted our solicitor in order to put in a bid, as in Scotland houses are mainly bought by a sealed bid arrangement, he informed me that it was a very popular area, so I would need to put in a fairly good bid, he suggested that an offer of £30,000 over and above the asking price, that should clinch the deal, as we wanted the house, I put in an offer of £36,000 above the asking price, however it was not to be, somebody had offered even more, it was around this time that people were offering silly money for properties.

In Scotland the way houses are bought and sold is by this sealed bid procedure, where each prospective purchasers bid, offers over a certain price, let us say that a house is for sale for £300.000, the property is then put up for sale at offers above £300,000, your bid above that asking price is put in a sealed envelope, as are any other bids on that property by other prospective purchases, these sealed bids are then opened in the presence of the solicitors representing their clients and it is usually the highest bid that clinches the deal.

This procedure seems to be somewhat better for the seller than the buyer as it can lead to great disappointment and uncertainty, as one has not really got a clue what to offer in order to be absolutely certain of a successful purchase, it is also open to abuse, in the event of there being only one bid made. I was informed by one solicitor, that a solicitor could well have two sealed bids available, one high priced bid in one pocket and a lower one in the other pocket, if when he arrives at the office where the bids are opened and he is made aware that there are no other bids in, he will reach in his pocket containing the lower sealed bid and offer that in order to seal the deal.

It was very important that we were able to get settled as quickly as possible as Lucy was going to have to change schools due to her age, having to leave primary school/ middle school and attend high school, so after much discussion about all of the uncertainty of purchasing a house in Scotland at that time, we decided that we would move back home to East Anglia, where one could usually offer slightly below the asking price and a reasonably quick deal could normally be done, signed and sealed without all of this sealed envelope business.

Lucy had absolutely no problems with a move to East Anglia all she ever wanted was to be with us, the dogs and the cat and she would be happy.

As usual I went on my own to look for a property to buy, Hollie once again seemed to trust me implicitly when it comes to the buying of a new house, it was a long journey some six hundred and fifty miles, even so, I do enjoy driving and on this occasion I was heading home, unfortunately my mum and dad had both passed away, as had Hollies parents, on previous visits I would stay at my parents home, now my very first port of call is to visit mum and dads grave which are situated in the churchyard of the village where I spent most of my childhood, it's always a bit sad, I loved them both and its also a great shame that they never got to meet our Lucy, they would have loved her to bits and she would have loved them.

Oh! If only I could put the clock back. I pulled up the weeds around mum and dads gravestone, gave the area a good clean up and sadly I had to say goodbye.

I then proceeded to look for a new house that we could turn into our new home, I looked over the next few days at around thirty different houses and bungalows in Norfolk concentrating in and around the Broads area, I was finding it very difficult to find a suitable property most of the houses available to buy had extremely small bedrooms.

In a great many of the houses I found, the only wall in the bedrooms where one could stand a free standing wardrobe, had in that wall the only window in the room, so if you were too place a wardrobe there in front of the window the only place where it would fit in the room, all natural light and ventilation would be gone, many of these bedrooms also had another problem when a decent sized bed was put in the bedroom, one had to walk sideways ducking ones head right down to be able to get in the bed, due too the narrow gap on either side of the bed and the slope of the ceiling in most modern homes nowadays they appear to be built in this strange head bashing or back wrenching fashion, in order to get into bed, in others if you sit up in bed you hit your head on the ceiling or a low beam, what an odd, bizarre way to design and then build a house.

Not for us, I knew that Hollie would not like a house built like that as we have a couple of large Italian free standing wardrobes, which we have had for many years which I know Hollie would never part with, in fact I always travel with my trusty tape measure, just to make sure that Hollies wardrobes will fit in the bedrooms, would I or could I be the first person to not buy a house because the wife's wardrobes would not fit in the bedrooms?

And barn conversions to us are a real No!No! They were built for animals not humans, they more often than not have bare brick walls and huge timber beams way out of reach without the use of a very long ladder these bricks and beams pose an almost impossible task to keep them clean, if you brush your hand along one of these beams they are usually caked with dirt and cobwebs, the same goes for the brickwork, it is usually filthy and due to the abnormal very high ceilings right up too the top rafters the heating bills must be mind boggling, the heating of masses of open, often unused space.

Another very important thing, was that I could find a house with the right school for Lucy nearby, we also didn't want to live beside a main road, because of traffic noise and exhaust pollution and we definitely didn't want a mobile phone mast nor electricity pylons near to the house, otherwise we would be jumping out of the frying pan into the fire.

I seemed at that point as if I had exhausted the estate agents supply of houses for sale, other than the houses I looked at, all they had left on their books were teeny cottages, at around the time that I was looking, houses throughout the country were selling like hot cakes.

I persevered and kept searching, I just drove the car around village after village looking for 'For Sale' boards, I done this for a couple of days, at last my patience and persistence were rewarded.

I found in a pretty village an architect designed house that seemed to be worth a look, it was a very modern quirky looking house, I stopped knocked on the door and asked the owner if I could possibly have a look around, I said that I would come back later if it was not convenient, he said "Come on In and have a look around,"

I first of all got out my trusty tape measure, and I asked him if I could measure the space in the bedrooms where I could fit these wardrobes, he obliged. They would fit in perfectly with tons of room to spare, in fact the master bedroom was enormous. I then looked at the rest of the house, it wasn't really to my taste and it also left a lot to be desired regarding cleanliness, but I could very quickly spot the potential and viewed it in such a way that I could see it in my minds eye after Hollie and me had cleaned it up and then put our mark on it. It was one of those houses where you had to ignore and look beyond its current state, the structure of the house all seemed in a good state of repair, except probably the drains and swimming pool needing some urgent attention.

Hollie and myself have never had a surveyor to look over any house that we have ever purchased, in the event that anything does need to be done, we use the money often many hundreds of pounds or even thousands that we save on the surveyors fees to help us carry out the work that needs doing, after all just how many surveyors have looked at the average house over the years, certainly on many houses several times, as on average people move house every seven years. So ask yourself just how many times are these houses surveyed?

That would mean that a fifty year old house has typically been surveyed on average seven times during its lifetime. And these surveyors seem to have so many get out clauses, like couldn't check the floors as carpets laid laid, couldn't check if chimney correctly supported as work carried out and camouflaged by a dodgy builder, couldn't see this or that because it was not visible.

We never buy thatched houses, nor houses built on a flood plain, nor those near a river, be very wary of newly built houses, they are very often full of hidden problems. Some newly built houses near us had to have their roof tiles completely removed as the now bankrupt builder failed to put in any insulation, they were covered by these so-called 10 year guarantees, they took months and months to pay up and get the faulty work rectified, one of the owners is still waiting after 3 years to get it sorted, having to employ a solicitor to sort out the mess, so buyers beware!

I gained my experience at looking for any problems with houses when I worked for a Local Authority for several years.

Some good advice given to me many years ago by an elderly canny man, he gave me this excellent advice, I have never forgotten it,
'Never look down at a house, always look up at a house,' that should invariably save you from any flooding problems, even so, check that the area is not prone to flooding, because even if your house is on a hill or incline, you still need to be able to get to your home.

The garden of the quirky house, it had a large garden, that was pretty much a blank canvas it was mainly laid to lawn, I immediately thought that I could soon use the rotavator to turn over the soil, add some well rotted horse manure it would then be absolutely perfect for growing my vegetables with plenty of room left over for a flower garden and lawn area for

Hollie and good sized bit would be left over for Lucy to have a play area and a chunk of garden.

The outlook from the garden was superb, at the top end of the garden were panoramic views over towards the distant sea, there was also a good view of a distant old fashioned windmill, and the house was right next door to the village church separated from it by a six foot high brick and flint wall all covered in ivy, it was delightful.

I then called on the neighbours to ask about the area, they all gave good reports, however, a decent school, they said was about eight miles away, I immediately thought that there was going to be a need for dads taxi service, I didn't relish the thought, however, they informed me that it was not a problem because a school bus picked up the local children just a very short walk away from the front gate of the house.

There was also another treat in store for Lucy, I phoned Hollie and Lucy to tell them all about the house that I had found, they both sounded very excited as I was telling them all about the house and garden, I then said to Lucy, winding her up, "I don't know if you are going to like it Lucy because it has got an indoor heated swimming pool," the excitement on the other end of the phone said it all, this was the one, all I had to do now was agree on a price with the owner, then I visited the estate agents office and a local solicitor and the deal was done.

The house in Scotland sold very quickly, however the house purchase in East Anglia was having a few problems, the solicitor dealing with the purchase was an elderly man and he started to get things seriously wrong, especially dates, to get him to understand the proposed date of moving was a nightmare, I had to write to him several times, stressing the correct date of purchase and the moving in date *in bold red ink*, because the dates he was writing and confirming to me were always around a month in difference from the true agreed date of purchase and moving in date.

I was getting a little concerned, as when one sells a house in Scotland that is it, there is no turning back, you have to move out, in England one can back out of a deal at the very last moment, in fact almost right up to the day of sale or purchase, in our case being in Scotland we would have to get out of the house on the agreed selling date.

Move Number Five

The removal date arrived two huge trucks were at our front gate, in fact the removal men had been at our home for three days prior to the move packing all of our household items in boxes, we all got stuck in and helped, including Lucy, she helped to pack some of her toys and books.

Hollie as usual became the tea lady supplying the removal men with copious amounts of tea and their favoured chocolate digestive biscuits for a whole four days, three days too pack our goods and chattrels in boxes and a further day to put all of the boxes in the trucks, finally they were loaded, we said our goodbyes and have a safe journey to the men, then off the first truck went heading for East Anglia, the second truck was just about to leave, in fact we were just saying our goodbyes "Have a good and safe journey and we will meet you again in a couple of days."

We then received an urgent phone call from our solicitor in England, "Don't move it's all gone pear shaped," the owner of the property in East Anglia had now decided that he didn't want to move, I said to the solicitor, "But I have paid you in full, its my house"in fact it wasn't as I mentioned earlier people selling their house in England can and do back out at the very last minute, I immediately informed the removal men to stop the truck already on its way to England and turn around and put all of our goods into storage and do the same with the goods inside the truck outside of our front door.
We were in fact at that moment homeless, we have had some ups and downs in our life, but I can honestly say that we had never been homeless before, I do not often get angry, but on this occasion I did get a little bit upset, thinking that we had actually paid in full for a house in East Anglia yet it wasn't ours, the money was in fact now in the hands of our solicitor, stuck in their clients account.

The House in Scotland was no longer our property, we had no alternative but to lock the door then pointed our car loaded with Hollie, Lucy and myself plus two dogs and a cat, for an all night drive down towards East Anglia, what the future held we had no idea. We drove all night stopping every now and then at motorway service stations to let the dogs have a little run around, also for us to have a cup of tea and stretch our legs, it felt like forever, Lucy kept on saying "Are we nearly there dad," we finally arrived in Kings Lynn at around seven a.m in the morning, we stopped to have an early breakfast, at that point we were about fifty odd miles from our destination, after breakfast we resumed our journey arriving at about nine o clock, we then visited lots of estate agents to see if we could find another house to buy, nothing suitable was available.

I was at this point getting a little concerned, there were the six of us, Hollie, Lucy and myself our two dogs and a cat, I got to thinking where on earth are we going to live at such short notice, I was really regretting that I had sold our motor home a few months earlier.

Lucy came up with the bright idea of us trying to hire a holiday cottage, however, being July in a popular holiday area, the chances were that these would all be fully booked, I also thought about staying in a hotel or a bed and breakfast place, but then I thought to myself who is likely to take the three of us and three animals, it would take a miracle.

Just as we were thinking that it was going to be impossible to find a place to stay, we arrived at a small market town, where we found a small estate agency office, the staff were extremely helpful and went out of their way to try and help us, after we told them what had happened to us.

Firstly they went through their whole stock of houses to buy, there was nothing at all suitable, then they started to look through their records to look for places that we might hire or rent.

They then contacted a whole load of people on the telephone. All they were getting was No! No! No! We thought that we were out of luck, then suddenly the lady said; "Will a holiday chalet do, its on a small park, its not very big, will that do" We all shouted out; Yes! Yes! Yes!, I then said "Anything will do," she then made arrangements for us to see the owner after explaining to him that we had the animals and we had been landed in this awful predicament, we said our thank you's.

We then proceeded to the chalet park, the owner was a lovely guy, saying that he was very pleased to help us and we could have the chalet for a week, after that it was booked up to other people.

It was just around the corner from the estate agent, it was a nicely kept site with around forty of these little chalets all separated by neatly cut grassed areas, it was also near and handy to the centre of the town.

The accommodation was very small, however, it was spotlessly clean, we were extremely grateful at the very least we now had a little home and a bed for a week.

Firstly we unpacked what little we had in the car, then the first job was to take the dogs for a walk around the site, meanwhile Hollie had put the kettle on, we then all had a very welcome cup of tea and a slice of Hollies homemade sponge cake which she had prepared earlier in Scotland, then we all relaxed for a while, that done the trick, we all felt a whole lot better after that, in fact it was quite exciting in a strange sort of way, with all of us being crammed in this little chalet with our dogs Digby, Sophie and Sooty the cat, not having a clue what we were going to do in seven days time. I later went to the local fish and chip shop and bought what must be the best fish and chips that we have ever tasted, we all sat down and ate them at the table, they were absolutely delicious.

Our cat Sooty was a bit of a problem, if the door of the chalet was opened for just a second, she would run out, it was difficult to watch her for every second, I had to purchase a new collar and lead for her and treat her just as if she was a dog, otherwise she may well have got lost, she didn't like being on a lead one little bit, cats are a bit of a law unto themselves, the dogs were absolutely no problem at all as they were used to going on holiday with us.

More good news came, the owner of the chalet contacted us and said that he had just received a cancellation for the two weeks following the end of our booking, would we like to book those two weeks, we gladly said 'Yes' that then immediately gave us a bit of breathing space, so although things were not perfect, they were now very much better than when we had first arrived.

Nevertheless, it was now very important to sort out what went wrong with our house purchase, I was not a happy bunny, the estate agent through whom we were purchasing the house, was of no help whatsoever, a hard luck old mate sort of attitude, these things happen, the solicitor did not seem to know if it was Christmas or Easter, I was told by his boss that unfortunately he was not very well, I wondered why on earth he was left in charge of arranging a house purchase for a client?

The manager then said that he would be taking over our case and try and sort things out. It transpired that the owner of the house we wished to purchase, still wanted to sell his house, but, he had to find another property for himself before he could move out.

It Felt A Bit Like We Were On A Holiday

I gave the owner of the house, the agent and the solicitor one week to sort it out, in the meantime we knuckled down to living in our little chalet, it was not as bad as we had first thought that it would be, in fact we went on a few short trips, mainly looking in estate agents windows to try and find another house that we could purchase quickly in the event these unreliable vendors selling the house let us down once more, even so, we started to worry just a little bit because at the end of the first week staying in the chalet, there was still no definite concrete good news, it was looking as if we would definitely have no choice other than to look urgently for somewhere else suitable to rent or buy.

Finally we got the call that we were all waiting for from the solicitor, he said that the sale could go through in around ten days time, that was if all went well, on the Wednesday of that week.

I thought however at this point that it would not be wise to arrange for our furniture to arrive from Scotland on that day as things still seemed to be up in the air and enormously uncertain, as it might not all happen, the couple selling the house were both school teachers, I was very annoyed at this, thinking that people who teach children jolly well ought to be more thoughtful on the way that they are treating other people, messing them around, they should surely set a fine example for the children they teach. I guess in this day and age this old saying comes to the fore; 'Self first, Self last, anything else left over Self can have it.'

We continued on living in the chalet, relaxing a bit at times by going for some enjoyable walks down by the river, Broadland is a remarkably pretty area, with its array of holiday boats and cruisers, there's wildlife in abundance as the various creatures can get away from man in the vast expanses of reed beds and lots of hidden inaccessible areas of woodland and immense areas of boggy wetland, in these delightful areas you will find herons, ducks, swans, kingfishers, bitterns, great crested grebes, marsh harriers, water voles the rare swallowtail butterflies, damsel flies and many more gems of the insect, bird and animal world.

When one considers that the Broads are all made up of lake like often vast areas of water which are named broads, these are all joined together by rivers, the broads are mainly man made, they were dug out in the past by peat diggers, the peat was heaped up and allowed to dry, when dry, it was burnt on open fires to heat peoples homes, it gives out a gentle heat, without creating a lot of smoke to keep people warm in those bygone days, it was also used as a packing material for stored fruit and vegetables in boxes to preserve them over long periods of time and to protect the vegetables from winter frosts.

The history of the quaint little Broadland villages is well worth exploring, each little village invariably had its own church, some with round towers other square, some of the churches are massive for the small communities that they served, many of these were built when the areas were hugely wealthy, the wealth was made from sheep, the wool was woven into cloth a famous one just outside of Broadland was Worstead, to this day there are some old yesteryear looms inside the church. There I go getting carried away by our pretty surroundings and history, when I had far more important things that I ought to be concentrating on, we were still homeless.

The Wednesday, our house entry day arrived, the time to gain entry was according to the solicitor, twelve o clock mid-day, he said that everything had gone through, we all turned up at the house bang on twelve o clock all of us were very excited, because, despite all of our problems everything seemed to have been sorted out satisfactorily, sadly we were to have our hopes dashed, there was nobody there, we peered through the windows the house was still pretty much filled up with furniture, we waited for around an hour, not a soul turned up, we went off to a local cafe and had a bite to eat.

Hollie and Lucy both looked a bit down in the dumps and the dogs were looking at us with sad eyes as if to say, will we ever be settled?

In fact at that point, we had all had enough, if this purchase were to fall through yet again we would really be in deep trouble, homeless, the chalet was only available up until the coming Saturday and our furniture was still in storage some six hundred and fifty miles away, I started to think, will it be possible for us all to find a hotel that would take us all in, or would we end up having to put Digby and Sophie in kennels and Sooty in a cattery. I even got to thinking that if all else fail I might have to invest in a tent.

We called at the house again at three o clock, alarm bells were ringing in my head, there was once again nobody there, we waited for about thirty minutes still nobody came, I took the family back to the chalet and contacted the solicitor, he just said to me that everything had gone through and there was nothing that he could do.

I then called back to the house around five o clock; At last! There were a couple of cars in the driveway, I could see through the window that there was still a lot of what looked like junk and rubbish still in the house, there was an old mattress thrown out into the front driveway, I thought to myself now calm down, I might add I was not in my best frame of mind, I rang the doorbell, they both came to the door, I asked them very politely for the keys of the house, I waited a while then very sheepishly they came up with a whole load of keys, I then asked them if that was all of the keys to the house, they replied 'Yes' I then said to them, "Now would you please mind getting out of my house," after about ten minutes they did, they got in their cars and that was the last I ever saw of them.

I was over the moon, I very quickly went inside. My excitement soon subsided, they had left the house in an absolutely, terrible filthy condition, there were even big piles of dog mess in several rooms, the drains and toilets were not working properly as I had earlier expected, they were in fact almost completely blocked up with excrement and huge balls of coagulated washing powder residue and cooking fat.

The house was not on the mains sewage system rather it had septic tank drainage system, we had often had these systems before and if maintained and cleaned our regularly around once a year they usually work perfectly well, and are not a problem, it soon became pretty obvious to me that they had been having problems with the drains for months or probably years, I would have to sort that out later on.

I was extremely disappointed at the way they had left the house, nevertheless, looking on the bright side, it was only muck and filth we could roll up our sleeves and with some elbow grease we could eventually sort it out, the great thing was, I was enormously pleased to have the keys safely in my hand. Not to be downhearted I went back to the chalet and told Hollie and Lucy what condition the house had been left in and we all decided that as it was now getting late, we would all get to bed and make an early start in the morning and get it sorted out.

The next morning we got up early then went to the house, I was very surprised that despite all of the muck and filth, they both actually liked the place, Hollie like myself could see quite clearly the potential by looking beyond what it looked like at that moment. I did feel a little bit ashamed bringing my family into such a filthy house, I was very grateful to think that I had a very understanding, helpful and loving wife.

We all worked extremely hard that first day, we cleared all of the junk out of the house, ripped up all of the filthy old carpets, making an enormous heap of them in the front driveway, I couldn't get a skip that day but I ordered one to be delivered as soon as possible, I rang the removal company, who were very good, saying that they could have one truckload there on the Saturday the other truck load would be delivered in around three weeks time, I was happy with that.

Following a hard days cleaning, using lots of bleach and other cleaning products, we went back to the chalet to sleep nights until the Saturday morning when we had to vacate the holiday chalet, we managed on vegetarian takeaway meals, we continued on with the cleaning of the house, going through every room in turn.

There was a bit of a funny story, one morning a chap in a large green van stopped at the gate of our new house, he said that he had just purchased a brand new van, he then asked me if he could have a bit of the old carpet from the heap that laid in the front driveway, he wanted it for the back of his new van, he explained that it didn't have any carpet in the rear of the van when he bought it, I said "Certainly take as much as you want, but, you will need to have it cleaned first," he then said "It will be ok"

He then proceeded cutting very carefully a bit of this filthy old carpet to size, I could smell the pong as he was fitting it, there was a really awful stench, I said to him "Would you like some more."He declined my offer, he said a big "Thank You" he then went on his way absolutely delighted, I can only hope that he bought a can of air freshener stuff or some pegs, at least that reduced the size of the heap of filthy old carpets just a weeny bit, we all had a good belly laugh over that.

It was then all hands on deck we thoroughly cleaned the whole house again several times using masses of disinfectant and yet more bleach to finally eradicate all of the awful miasma, I then realised that an awful lot of the smells were emanating from the blocked drains, so I purchased a couple of sets of rods and pushed them through the drains, that did improve the situation just a little, but I was going to have to get in a specialised drain company in at a later date.

We chucked all of the rubbish into a skip that had just arrived, the house then started too look and smell a whole lot better.

The furniture arrived as promised on the Saturday and we were fortunate that most of it went into the large double garage that was attached to the house, that enabled us to move it bit by bit into the house over several weeks, with a bit of help from tradesmen we painted every room in the house, as each room was painted and new carpets laid, we were then able to furnish each room in turn with furniture from the garage moved into the redecorated rooms. Hollie sorted out where all of the furniture and household items were going to go, she always did have a knack of knowing just where something looks at its best.

I eventually had to get a specialised firm in to completely replace the faulty septic tank system, as the original one there was no longer fit for purpose. The second load of furniture finally arrived after a few weeks, I was not very happy because our prized conservatory plants arrived with most of them dead, having been in storage, it was quite obvious from their condition that they had not been watered.

It was also now the time for Lucy to go to school as the summer holidays were now over, I took Lucy to her new school on the first few days in order for her to get used to her new surroundings, I found everybody to be very helpful and friendly, we met the headmaster a tall blonde headed very friendly man, he welcomed Lucy to the school with a warming smile, she then met a whole host of other teaches, Lucy looked a little forlorn, when I had to leave her with all of these new people who she didn't know. She settled in very quickly, saying that she liked it.

Lucy was able to get to know lots of new schoolmates very quickly as she started to go to school on the bus with lots of local children, the school bus picked her up almost right outside of our front gate.
By this time the dogs Digby and Sophie had settled down well they were enjoying their walks along the many footpaths that we had discovered near to the house, and Sooty was really enjoying the garden as there was an abundance of different flowering shrubs all around the garden boundary, she would spend hours looking around under these hiding places in between lazing in the sun, its nice to see a happy contented cat.

The swimming pool was in a very poor state of repair, so I got a pool company that specialised in this work to re-tile the pool, we also had a new oil boiler fitted to heat the house and the pool plus we had fitted four new solar panels on the roof to help heat the swimming pool.
Once the pool was fixed and looking like new, it didn't take Lucy very long before she learned to swim and she often invited her friends round to join her in the pool.
The house took us about a year of really hard work to sort out.
I then with a bit of help from Lucy started seriously working on the garden, I had previously just kept it tidy cutting the hedges and lawn, now we started to plant loads of fruit trees and bushes, blackcurrant's, gooseberries, red currants, raspberry canes, apples, plums and pears, we then purchased a cedar wood greenhouse planting that up with lettuces, tomatoes and cucumbers, Lucy helped a lot, I do believe that she was taking to gardening and was enjoying it now that she is now getting a little older, that pleased me no-end.

Our house was adjacent to the local village church, bell ringing was of course on a Sunday and bell ringing practice on a Thursday evening for about an hour, it was particularly interesting to hear the new bell ringer over the months, going from what one can only describe as dire, all out of tune, really clashing sounds, then slowly but surely he got the hang of it, he got better and better, finally, he mastered it, it became music to ones ears, very melodious and hugely enjoyable, we all enjoyed sitting out in the garden on fine summer Thursday evenings listening to the various tunes.

Lucy was improving greatly in all manner of things, she was now a good letter writer, working on a computer she was excellent, absolutely putting Hollie and myself to shame, we asked her constantly. 'How do we do this or that, in a flash she would tell us and show us how to do it, we would say 'Not so quick' I am now convinced from watching Lucy, that having a go when working on a computer was by far the best policy, previously our thinking was that we were afraid of getting something wrong and mess it all up. Lucy if she was not certain what to do with this or that, she gets stuck in and has a go, if at first it's not quite right, she perseveres and 'Bingo' problem solved. She has in fact given me a lot of advice on the use of using a computer in the writing of this story.

Additionally as time went by we noticed that Lucy had started to take a very keen interest in cooking, she would ask mum if she could help, Hollie would always oblige and was always keen to pass on tips and recipes to help Lucy, who would always put on her pretty little apron, then search through her mums thousands of recipes for all kinds of culinary creations and then she would be away, in fact she was fast becoming a very good cook and a dab hand at turning out all kinds of delicious cakes, pasta dishes, biscuits, pizzas, Welsh cakes, butterfly cakes and mum taught her how to make sponge cakes which she fills with jam or cream, she really was growing up to enjoy home cooking, celebrity chefs and cooks watch out you soon might have some competition.

I might add that she always helps her mum to clean up afterwards, I keep out of the way, being her dad, I like to clean up by eating her choice offerings.
Lucy also liked to watch those TV chefs and buying cookery books, I have lost count of how many she now has.

She excelled at school, became a prefect and she always had a good report, one teacher said to me that "She wished that all the children in her school were as well behaved and polite as our Lucy" That made me feel ten feet tall and an unbelievably proud dad.

I very often sit and contemplate on the tens of thousands of children in care, I would have liked to have helped them all, that was not possible, however what was possible was to highlight their plight, so that maybe others could read our story and perhaps it might spur them on to want to adopt a child. If our story helps just one child escape the awful system of being thrown from pillar to post, either in foster care or in a children's care home then it would all have been worthwhile, so from this point on I will highlight what I genuinely feel needs very urgently needs to be done to help children like our Lucy.

Decent People Who Would Make Fine Parents Are Being Turned Away In Droves

The care system in the UK needs urgently to drastically change, many decent people who would make fine parents are being turned away in droves, we must never forget that tens of thousands of children are languishing in State care, many of those prospective adopters who are being turned away can give these children a loving home.

One only has to look at the recent reported cases of young girls who were living in a children's care home and were supposed to be looked after by the care staff in those homes.

Reports clearly show that there was a complete and utter lack of care, it was highly likely that if the children's home care staff and social services personnel had shown a bit of loving care for these girls and listened intently to their horror stories of rape in the early stages of being told and had they checked on just why these girls were going missing, their ordeal need not have happened, it was reported that these girls went missing for days on end from these children's care homes. Do these people looking after these children really understand what the word care actually means, Just who was in charge of caring for these defenceless children.

In just one year, it was reported that one girl went missing over one hundred and twenty times, one could reasonably ask, were they not missed by the people responsible for their care? It is patently obvious that these girls were not being cared for in an appropriate manner by the people who were entrusted to care for them and who had a duty of care towards these vulnerable girls, I would even go as far as saying that these so-called care staff were guilty of wilful neglect, because of their total lack of care allowing these girls to be befriended and groomed by members of a gang who it is alleged gave them alcohol, gifts and drugs, which it is fairly obvious led to these vulnerable girls being sexually abused consistently over many months by this gang of men.

The girls on numerous occasions it is alleged mentioned to their carers the fact that they were being violently raped by these men, however no action was taken at that time against these men

It would appear that nobody cared one jot about these girls, if they did wouldn't they have had the decency to have reported these girls as missing.

119

If a child entrusted to our care was ten minutes late, alarm bells would start ringing, these girls went missing time and time again over many months, one has to ask are these people entrusted to the care of these girls still in their jobs? If they are, those who didn't care for these children, they should in my opinion be instantly relieved of their duties and should never again be allowed anywhere near such vulnerable children.

And we now learn, children are not just shunted around foster carers by social workers, children are also shunted around children's care homes very often miles from their roots, one young girl was moved around different children's care care homes a total of some thirteen times in a two year period, let us all ask ourselves, would we like to move house thirteen times in the space of two years, this girl urgently needed a stable home living with people that she could rely on, share her problems with, she also needs love and affection, how on earth is this young girl ever going to be able to live a normal life, she was being treated abominably.

I looks as if many people who own and run these children's care homes seem to be accountable to no-one, it is alleged that even people who should be in a position to know where these homes are situated are prevented under the data protection act from getting information on where these children's care homes are, what children are housed in them and even who is caring for them. Many people, have expressed the view that on trying to get details of where these homes are situated, who is housed in them, how many, boys, girls, ages, this information appears to be a total secret and these people have stated that they were coming up against a brick wall of total silence. It would seem that the secret system matters far more than the children in it, it is truly disgusting.

Note what the word care actually means, according to the dictionary:
To care is to be anxious, to be inclined, to be concerned, to mind, to have a liking or fondness for, to provide, to look after and watch over, to protect, tending, show consideration, show regard, supervision, guardianship.

I hardly dare think what would have happened to our Lucy, if we hadn't have come along and adopted her, she could well have ended up in one of these secret care homes with nobody being allowed to know where she was it could have been anywhere in the country, and very sadly she would have been shown no heartfelt love because there would have probably been no-one who cared about her,what an awful disgusting state of affairs.

How much better it would be, in fact it's shouting at me, to place these young children in loving family homes with caring parents as these seemingly disastrous places cannot ever take the place of a loving caring family home with the child living as part of that family, having parents, this has got to be infinitely light years far more superior for these children than being stuck in these children's care homes with a load of carers who it would appear that many are not giving these children the loving care that they need.

Alright there would be some problems for some of the children taken out of care, everything will not be all roses, but we have to give these children a chance, a fair crack of the whip, anything has to be better than putting these children who desperately need help in a secret children's care home. Even Government members agree with this. What was said by one of them in the year 2000. Note carefully what one of them said;

"No matter how good a care home is, it isn't as good as having a loving family! Who could possibly not agree with that statement, yet that was said years ago, and absolutely nothing seems to have changed since then. Let us have a look at what was said some thirteen years later as follows:-
In 2013 in a Parliamentary question this was stated;
'Clearly it is shocking that so many children are living under the control of the State, but are NOT being brought up in families'...... Familiar words.

We all know what they are saying loud and clear, that children would be far better off living with a loving family rather than being stuck in a care home or some other forms of State care.

Its a very sad world, when we have those, who have the power to change things for the better for these children, are pontificating about what needs to be done. They know full well what needs to be done, so why don't they jolly well get on with it?

There are now more children, not less in State care, at the last count it was said too be around 67,000. This enormous figure in recent years has become stagnant, despite a few children being placed with families, more and more are being taken into care topping up the numbers again, Whatever good is that?

Various reports have stated that Local Authorities pay typically an average of up too Four thousand pounds per week (£4000) per child at the present time to house these children in these care homes, that in itself, if true, is a national disgrace, who on earth is getting all of this cash for not caring correctly for all of these children in children's care homes with many of these homes falling way behind the set minimum standards, it is high time

that the secrecy surrounding these often awful places is made totally trans-
parent, why is there all of this hiding of the the truth, could it be that there
is some kind of secret miasmal, machiavellian cover up going on?
If there are devious unmentionable secrets going on within these
children's care homes,? They need urgently too be uncovered and exposed
forthwith no delays or excuses or have we got to wait another thirteen
years for some other person to tell us what we already know, that the
children in these many uncaring children's care homes would be far better
off living with a loving caring family, rather than be housed in secret care
homes where nobody knows where they are situated, nor who is housed
within them, with the exception of those who are in on the secrets,
whoever they might be?
After all the year is 2014 anyone would think that we were living in the
dark ages with all of this injustice being done to these young vulnerable
people in the so-called democratic UK.
It would seem that even some members of parliament, if it is to be believed
what we read in various reports, have zero access to any knowledge of
where these care homes are situated? Who owns them? How many
young children are being housed in them, in a modern society how on
earth is this being allowed to happen? It is not only wrong it is morally
repugnant.
The sooner the powers that be stop this absolute nonsense, come clean and
let the public know why they are doing this, and just what is going on
regarding these children's care homes, why they are needed? when there
are thousands and thousands of families who would dearly love to help
these children by giving them a good home, yet such people are being
rejected by social services to carry out this valuable role. One could rightly
ask, could it possibly be that all of this horrific scheme of things is devised
for other purposes?

These Children Need Urgently To Be Placed With A Family Who Can Help Them

I must confess that I am very deeply troubled by the very thought of these
children being in such a horrific situation, there must be somebody who
has the power and the common decency to stop this appalling so-called
children's care home shambles, these children need urgently to be placed
with a family who can help them, OK there will be a few who will probably
never accept any help, however there must be many, many thousands of
these children who would give their right arm to be loved, to be shown that
we, the people of this country really do care what is happening to these
children. And do not forget that these children hopefully or should I say

122

regretfully have social workers, who should be aware of their plight, why are they not properly caring or overseeing the plight of these children.

The bulk of social services social workers that Hollie and myself have met and had to deal with had little or no idea on how to correctly help these very vulnerable children, they seem to be just like numbers to them, in fact I remember one saying to Hollie, 'I couldn't possibly adopt one of these children' the whole adoption, fostering and children's care home business is in my opinion not fit for purpose.

Let me give you one or two examples as to why I say this;
It was reported that one young boy was taken into care, he was then over a period of around fourteen years moved ninety six times to live with different foster parents, each time, why? That must have been as near to mental torture as one could possibly get.

In another similar case, a young boy in this case was moved around and lived with a total of seventy five foster carers over a thirteen year period, it makes one wonder just how many changes of social workers these two boys experienced during all of these movements, it must have been an enormous number, why didn't at least one of these social workers who were supposed to oversee the welfare and care of these boys recognise or spot the trauma that these boys must have been suffering and used their position to find a family to adopt him, there must have been many hundreds, if not thousands of people who would be up to the challenge, with perhaps a little help from social services.

All of this moving around must have caused great uncertainty in the lives of these two young boys causing them great emotional distress, they could well have suffered severe health and development damage from these experiences that they will never get over. After all a child is surely entitled to grow up with a loving family who can give that child some kind of normality in their lives.

If parents were to cause such gross emotional distress to their children it is very likely that social services would take their children into their awful discreditable care system. Yet that is exactly what these social workers are doing themselves, treating these children worse than very bad parents. Those in power continue to make noises and lots of promises on what they are going to do about these situations, but usually nothing actually happens and the children languishing in their care grow older resulting in many more harder to place children.

Various adoption agencies have newspapers or folders showing several photographs of children in care awaiting adoption. I remember well, along with Hollie spending many hours studying pictures of these scores of children from all over the UK, we must have spent a small fortune phoning the people who were overseeing the proposed placement for adoption of these children.

They Will Wreck Your House

A case in point, two little blonde girls, sisters, who both looked like little angels, who from memory must have been around five or six years of age, I telephoned the social worker regarding these two little girls, his loud immediate response was "Oh! You wouldn't want them, they are both sexually active on a regular basis," he then went into most graphic details, which I will not go into, I would think from his extremely negative attitude that these two little girls were never placed with adoptive parents, they in fact very urgently needed help, not condemnation in fact Hollie and myself were extremely surprised that such graphic details about individual children in care would be given out over the phone at such an early stage of an enquiry to people like us, as we were totally unknown to the people to whom we were talking.

Still others told us of children who were destructive, they will wreck your house, we were told, with others, they will destroy your marriage, every phone call we made to these people asking questions about these children, their answers were without exception always totally negative.
I was very aware that the facts had to be spelt out and be made known to people who wished to adopt a child, but this was all over the top, there was never one good word ever spoken about any of these children, who on earth I thought to myself is going to ever adopt these what were after all little children, needing an awful lot of help, they needed patient loving parents who could guide them and help them on their pathway of life, not this continual talking them down. It is no wonder that an awful lot of these children end up in children's care homes, but maybe that was the plan?

I notice a 1970s fashion has returned, apparently it is all the rage in America at the present time, children are now attending adoption parties where people can select the children they like, no wonder they are called 'A Cattle markets for kids' this crazy idea will be an absolute disaster as it is highly likely that certain children at these parties will always be overlooked by prospective adopters and this could be totally devastating for that child or children to be turned down several times, it is not fair and it certainly is not fun, it reminds one of former times when kids were literally put in a line and people would choose a child from that line, maybe the child chosen was better looking in these peoples eyes or maybe more chatty than other children it is none other than a children's fashion parade, that is certainly no way to start a lifelong relationship with a child, its rather like picking the prettiest puppy dog out of a litter. Shy children, less abled children or not so good looking children will likely be rejected in this totally silly speed dating for children idea.

The answer is not parties that might sound rather cool and trendy but they are not, rather they are cruel to the children who are not chosen, wouldn't it be a far better idea to choose some of the 22000 people who are turned down every year on average by social services, the bulk of these people *want to adopt a child,* it took Hollie and myself thirteen years to be chosen out of this huge amount of people who applied every year. Why?

Also this recently reported proposed database for adoption will be a total and utter failure, if it is overseen and run by the existing social workers, it is pretty likely that the powers that be will be using these people to run the show, if that is the case, it will be just like re-arranging the chairs on the Titanic as it was going under, it will be doomed to failure.
There is even talk of getting *top flight graduates* into the profession. Whatever that means? I do know what is urgently needed to run this new database, people with a genuine compassion for the job and above all people who love children, people who really care about righting the wrongs of just what is happening to these children, people with fire in their belly to want too get these children as quickly as possible into loving family homes.

I do not consider that *top flight graduates,* would have a clue about how to go about helping these young children, they will probably be more interested in their careers and promotion and wage packet, than they are about the future welfare of these children, they would be no different to most of the current lot of social workers who are often career minded. It is not an academic skill that's needed, its loving these children and the desire to help them.
Prospective adopters also need encouragement to want to help these often damaged children, our Lucy when she first arrived with us, had lots of problems and tantrums, she would, we were told rip the wallpaper off the walls of foster carers homes, why? She has told us since, because she didn't like the attitude of the foster carers, she even threatened to throw her social worker down the stairs, I cannot blame her, Joking apart, she has never threatened to throw Hollie or me down the stairs, also she has never

destroyed anything in our home, so we must have done something right, it is the way that these children are helped, treated and loved that is important.

Almost all of these children as a rule have some kind of problem, in most cases in my opinion it can usually be traced right back to a basic lack of love and kindness that should have been shown towards them, society is to blame, many of these children have been abused and neglected, they often mistrust grown ups, and rightly so, as a society we have badly let them down, they need urgently to feel valued, welcomed with open arms into our homes, so that they can then learn from those of us who love them and really do care about them, this would go on to help and teach them how to love and care for their own children when they become parents, getting them off this continuing, consistent merry-go- round of abuse and neglect.

The state, using local authority social services and some huge charities, have also very seriously let these children down, these children need urgently to be given stable homes, they need to be taken out of the hands of social workers, who are very obviously not up to the job, if they were there would not be all of these tens of thousands of children being carted around from pillar to post being housed temporarily with foster carer after foster carer.

Nor would there be thousands of children subjugated into very often grossly inadequate children's care homes, many of which do not even come up to basic guideline standards, these poor children do not have a clue where they will be the next day, let alone the next year, they need top priority Now! to be housed with loving families, who will care for them and treasure them, if you or I were treated like these often sadly neglected children, I hate to think how we would behave, if we all only wanted a perfect child, we could never have one, there is no such thing as a perfect child or a perfect match, there would have been no way that we would have adopted Lucy if we had only accepted a perfect child. There is an old saying, 'A person who never made a mistake, never made anything.'

This business of fostering these vulnerable children out to goodness knows who and where, is a complete shambles and an utter disgrace, as in Lucy's case the foster carer chain smoked all day long.

Lots of children are placed with scores of different foster carers all over the place, there is absolutely no doubt that many of these people really do care for the children they are looking after, and I applaud them for that.

Even so all children need a permanent long term forever loving home, not to be under the constant threat of just getting settled, only to be moved on again to another home full of strangers, for social services to keep on doing this is disgraceful.

I fully appreciate that some children do need to be looked after in short term care for a variety of reasons. I am here not referring to them, In fact I would like to say a big Thank you to the foster carers who look after these children for short periods until they can either be returned to their homes or indeed if it is the case be found new homes with loving families.

If we grown ups were stuck in a home with total strangers, either in foster care or in a children's care home, often many miles from our familiar territory, not knowing whether it was going to be for a couple of days, a week or several years, I am sure that we would not feel secure, as just when we had got used to a foster family or the children living with us in a children's care home, then along comes the social workers and like cattle they move us on to pastures new, by all of this upheaval we would probably never be able to form any long term friendship with anybody. I do not know about you but I personally would be terrified and upset, in fact, I would loath being in such a position.

Would any of us truthfully, feel like putting ourselves in these vulnerable children's shoes, I doubt it very much, we would probably feel lonely, losing all of our hope, despondent, feeling un-loved, sad, depressed, probably angry, thinking where next, will I like or get on with people at the next place where I am going to be put, it has to be grossly unfair to treat young people in such an inhumane, uncaring, inconsiderate, callous way. Yet that is exactly what these little ones are having to endure, often over and over and over again for years.

I reckon that the bulk of those 67000 children in State care could very easily be found loving homes very comfortably within the space of a very few years of years, as there are literally tens of thousands of prospective adopters who are turned away every year by social services, these people are a valuable asset to the State, they could save the government £Billions of pounds each year, if these people were allowed to adopt these children, just think, the bulk of the care homes could be shut down, this would then very obviously save many tens of thousands of pounds, if not £Millions in children's care home fees. The huge amount of money paid out to foster carers would virtually cease, and I would hate to think what the wages bill is for all of these social workers and their office staff, by reducing social services staff much more money could be saved.

These prospective adopters are like valuable gems, they want to be able to adopt these children, like us they do not want huge amounts of money for look after these children in fact we have never had one single penny from the State in the looking after Lucy with the exception that we received normal family allowance that anyone else with a child is entitled too, she is our daughter and we consider that it is our personal responsibility to look after and pay for her every need, others like us will look after them because of their love of children, if they do need a little financial help then there would be plenty left in the kitty to help them.

Social workers and especially their bosses need to be asked this question, just what is wrong with the 22,000 prospective adoptive parents on average that you turn away each year, I do not believe for one moment that amongst this large group of people that you cannot find a very sizeable number of very upright honourable people who would be very capable of looking after these children in a far better way than you are currently doing, they would dearly love to take care of the children who you are not caring for in a satisfactory manner, I speak from experience as my wife and myself went through an eleven year plus period of rejection, I now speak on behalf of others just like us who wish to adopt a child.

Some MPs are still saying things like, more needs to be done to recruit additional adoptive parents, that is absolute balderdash and rubbish, how about using the ones that are constantly being turned down, thousands of them every year?
The forgoing horror stories clearly show that the current system is definitely not working, the children are not being placed with families in satisfactory numbers, this is very clearly shown by the number of children in care has stagnated when it should be going down.
Those within the current adoption system urgently need to completely change their attitude, bring some fellow feeling, considerateness, affection, love and compassion into their work.

There is talk of nurses probably having to incorporate the word compassion written into their contracts, due to some appalling care by some in that profession, would it be a good idea, if it is not already there to the word compassion being included in the contracts of all those people who work for social services? It would be a reminder for them to then bring this quality to the forefront of their dealings with the children that they are entrusted to help, let us just contemplate on the meaning of that word.

It encompasses, mercy, kindness, tender-heartedness, fellow-feeling, benevolence, gentleness, leniency, commiseration, condolence, consideration, natural-affection, understanding, concern, and care.

Do you remember that we were told by our social worker right at the start of our journey to adopt a child, she said that 'These Children Do Not Respond to Love,' that we were naive to think that showing love to a child in care, would help, well I could now tell her with complete confidence, that she was grossly wrong, in fact her whole attitude towards her work was wrong, she was wrong to make such a statement to Hollie and myself, she very obviously lacked in her work that very important quality, Compassion!
We can now after all of these years with complete confidence say that the stance that she took on this, was misguided nonsense, showing love respect and compassion for these children, should have been the most important and essential part of her social workers job.
If these children have never been shown love because social workers state that it doesn't work with children in care, therefore, as these children have never been shown any kind of love from these social workers, how on earth are they ever going to understand whether or not these children will positively respond to love?

Without any shadow of doubt these children urgently need help, they desperately need to be loved by people who care, that is the area where the State needs to concentrate on, those social workers who think of these children in such a twisted way need urgently to be retrained, to learn how to be friendly, pleasant, gracious and show true love, kindness, trust, fellow feeling, mercy, tenderness, compassion and sorrow for all the sufferings that these young children are having to endure, if they cannot or will not try to excel in these qualities in their work towards these insecure unloved children, they need to be shown the door, urgently!!
There is talk of social workers needing new skills, forget the skills, if they do not know how to love these children, all the skills in the world will not help them one iota, its that something that is natural in a persons heart that they appear to have missing.

Alternatively the other answer is to hand over the whole failing adoption system to be run by *small caring charities*, where careers and money are not more important than these children's needs and the current disgusting adoption system is not more important than the children it is supposed to be caring for.

I understand that the State is talking about a huge funding for charity adoption agencies to be more involved in the adoption process, that will be ok, providing that it is not based on somebody making a huge amount of cash out of it, It is useless to keep on chucking more cash at these problems its compassion that's needed.

The State appears to be handing more and more adoption work over to these enormous charities, unfortunately this will definitely not work, the reason being is that these charities are putting large advertisements in newspapers to recruit staff at excessive salaries, encouraging so-called qualified staff to come out of social services to join them, whatever good is that, the government will be wasting huge amount of money funding these charities that will be run by the very self same people who are making a complete cock-up of the current adoption system.

It would also seem that charities are no longer charities, rather to me they seem to be huge tax avoiding businesses, so in the longer term the adoption system will be run by exactly the same staff as currently employed by local authority social services, except that they will all be on much higher salaries, working for a greedy charity whose main objective appears to be to make as much tax avoided cash as humanly possible. It is a recipe for disaster.

I am led to believe that the State already funds charities to the tune of hundreds of millions of pounds, yet charities still plead poverty, where may one ask is all of this cash going? Some is being wasted as follows:- We are currently seeing many charity executives getting a huge wage packet with loads of these executives getting £100,000 (One hundred thousand pounds a year)

Many are getting close to getting double that figure, is it any wonder they keep on asking in their television or newspaper advertisements, 'Give us a couple of quid a month, even at the £100,000' salary, very much the middle bracket of their huge wage packets, just think that it will take 50,000 (Fifty Thousand) of us sending off our couple of pounds to pay just this one persons salary.

I understand that one of these charity executives is said to earn£184,000 (One hundred and eighty four thousand pounds) a year, (That is far more than our Prime Minister gets for running the country.) That therefore means that a total of 92,000 (Ninety two thousand) people will have to send off their £2 (two pounds,) this will pay just this one mans wages, no doubt there are many more £thousands that will go to make up his expenses, none of that money is going to help the causes that you are giving your hard earned cash for.

Do these people think that they are bankers?

I for one have personally vowed never again to waste my cash by giving it to these overpaid executives who head these bottomless money box charities, I will be giving my donations willingly to *small local charities* and good causes or give to the local cats home, at least then I will be given the satisfaction of knowing that my contribution will be spent on the feeding and looking after a cat and not on a fat cat executive head of a charity who will trouser my money in his or her huge pockets.

Carefully note, I said *small charities*, I notice in many recent reports that even some of the cats and dogs larger charities are paying huge amounts money to the managers or executives to the detriment of the animals that they are supposed to be caring for.

Surely it is possible to find, dedicated kind people to run these charities for the love of the children or people or horses or cats and dogs or whatever the charity run is in aid of, who would willingly accept a far more modest salary, rather than them wanting these gross wage packets, then most of these enormous rewards given too these executives could be and should surely be spent on the task at hand, I would ask and there is no doubt many more people like me are raising the same question, just what is their motive? I know that these charities have many volunteers who do not get paid a bean, perhaps these greedy people running these charities should take a leaf out of their book, if not, they also should be shown the door.

Once again we speak from experience, the adoption agency the we had the pleasure of dealing with was a small charity run agency, who had the greatest pleasure in dealing with our quest to adopt Lucy, they were caring, kind, thoughtful and gracious towards the children entrusted to their care and towards Hollie and myself as prospective adopters.

Money nor donations were never ever mentioned, their motive was the job in hand to help people like us, not how much money can we possibly squeeze out of them, so that we can pay those running the show an enormous salary.

Their kindness certainly rubbed off on Lucy, she keeps in regular contact with them by letter or by card, they are a huge example to the human race on how it should be done.

An exception I would certainly make was the Barnardo's charity whose manager seemed to be far more interested in the décor and cleanliness of our home, thinking that our home was too clean and tidy, rather than what he should have been concentrating on! The future prospect of some poor child entrusted to their care being found a loving home! Hollie was quite upset by this tactless Barnardo's managers comments that he made during an assessment at our home saying; Its a bit clean and tidy isn't it"
This assessment of us and the evaluation of our home took around thirty minutes and from his comments, one could easily conclude that he wanted to place these children currently under Barnardo's care, in a shabby, dirty, unkempt home, his whole attitude in our opinion was grossly wrong.

Coincidentally, I remember well a personal chance encounter on my travels, I called at a house selling garden plants in pots on the side of the road, with an honesty box for payment, having selected a few plants for my garden, I dipped in my pocket and found that I did not have enough loose change to pay for them, resulting in my walking up to the front door of the house to pay, a man came to the door, I gave him a ten pound note, he said "Step inside and I will get you some change" we then got talking about gardening, then the conversation got around to adoption, he then told me that he had adopted some boys from Barnardo's.

I must say that I was astounded, the house was absolutely filthy, rubbish piled everywhere, I also noted that there was not a hand rail on the steep stairs leading up from the hallway to the upstairs rooms of the house.

I was not being nosy, its just that when I used to work years earlier for a local authority, in the housing department, it was part of my job to organise the mucking out dirty houses just like this one and to also look out for dangers within the houses before they were re-let out to new tenants and no hand rail on steep stairs was listed as a major hazard, hence my noticing that there was not one in situ here, I also noticed a tumbledown greenhouse in the garden which had lots of broken panes of glass, many dangerous shards of glass were exposed.

I remember thinking, how was he ever allowed to adopt Barnardo's children, he seemed a pleasant enough chap, even so, with his house and garden in such an unsavoury, unpleasant, dirty and dangerous condition, health and safety should surely have been an issue in this case, I would not have put my pet dogs in that house.

I have since written a letter to Barnardo's regarding our house being described by one of their managers as, It's a bit clean and tidy isn't it. We shortly afterwards got this reply.

BARNARDO'S

Thank you for your letter which was passed to me today, I am sorry to hear of your experiences with Bardardo's, I would have hoped that the staff at that time would have been able to communicate any concerns they might have had about your application in a more appropriate way, I appreciate that we are not now able to repair your experience of Bardardo's but your feedback is important to us as we continue to endeavour to recruit and prepare applicants to adopt vulnerable children, I will therefore ensure that the messages you give about over concern with the décor etc. are shared with our current adoption managers.
As you will appreciate it can be difficult to recognise peoples potential and I think adoption agencies are constantly endeavouring to learn from adoptive parents and adopted children/adults. As you suggest we do not always get things right, but Barnardo's belief in and commitment to vulnerable children encourages us to accept challenges and to endeavour to learn and do better.
I also think that we now have systems in place which improve the assessment, process, our managers are involved in more 'Second opinion' visits and there is more robust adoption panel regulations which allows prospective adopters greater representation. We are endeavouring to recruit adopters from a wide range of backrounds and different skills and have been consulting recently with a wide range of carers to ascertain their views on what we do well and what we might improve for the future.
I am pleased to hear about your successful adoption of your daughter and wish you and your family well.
Yours Sincerely.

My considered response to this charity Barnardo's reply letter is that the comments about learning to do better cannot hide the fact that they have been dealing with children's welfare for around one hundred and forty six years, if they have not been able to get most of it right in that number of years it is very sad.
To state that a prospective adopters house, is a bit clean and tidy for this charities children to live in with a loving family, beggars belief !

Society has badly let these vulnerable children down, they therefore need to be housed with a caring family in the cleanest of homes possible, we all owe it to them, it is not their fault for the situation that they find themselves in, a clean and safe environment for them is therefore paramount and essential to a child's well being and health, because in a dirty environment harmful to health, germs, harmful bacteria and mould can cause all kinds of health problems for children, chest problems, tummy bugs and asthma attacks, eye irritation, fungal infection, allergic reactions and headaches plus a whole host of other ailments.

Raising children in a filthy dirty home is classed as one of the worst forms of neglect, in fact such conditions are totally unsafe, these conditions can and do often result in children suffering from physical or even emotional problems.
In fact filthy home conditions are probably one of the main reasons why children are taken away from their birth parents and put into the care system and then put up for adoption in the first place, because those parents and their children, were living in squalor, dirt, mould and filth, if that was the case and the parents are warned that their children's health, safety and welfare are at stake and they make no attempt to clean up their home then it is highly likely that their children will be removed from that home, and rightly so.

So what then would be the sense of an adoption agency then attempting to place that child or children back into a very similar filthy, dirty, unclean environment, the child would automatically think that that is the way that people live, thus as they get older and have a family of their own, those children as they grow up, will also very likely allow their house to become filthy dirty as they would naturally assume that this was the way people live, they will then be on that familiar merry- go- round, it will probably go on and on, having their future children taken into the care system, therefore nothing would ever change.

These children in care have a human right to be brought up in the very best way that it is humanly possible, in this very sick society, common decency towards the welfare of these insecure, defenceless, vulnerable children is of the utmost importance.

If other people have been turned down in their endeavour to adopt a child for the same reasons that we were, that Barnardo's considered that their house was too clean and tidy, therefore they were not considered suitable to adopt a Barnardo's child, then that would have been a very sad day, not only for the family wanting to adopt a child, but also more importantly for the child or children who would have been denied the opportunity to become part of a caring loving family, living in a safe and clean and wholesome environment, if they were older children then their chance of being adopted might have never ever happened again.

Lucy's Health was Being Jeopardised Due To Filthy Home Conditions

In her early life our Lucy was in such a situation, her report said 'Lucy's health was being jeopardised due to filthy home conditions' resulting in Lucy being removed from her home and an order was issued to refuse any further contact with her birth parents.
Therefore the very least Hollie and myself could possibly do for our Lucy was to give her a spotlessly clean home to live in.

No doubt there will be someone who will read this and say, we adopted a child through Barnardo's and everything was fine, if that is the case, that is great news and we hope that you are experiencing great happiness, we are only pointing out what happened to us on our journey, if Barnardo's has now got its act together and learned to do better, that can only be good news, we have absolutely no axe to grind.

The only very important thing in our eyes is the welfare of all of those thousands and thousands of vulnerable children still in care, if Barnardo's are now making some kind of effort to place these children in clean homes with parents who take a lot of care regarding the child or children's health and well being, who could ask for more.

Thinking back Hollie and myself got to know several couples during the years in which we were trying to adopt a child, many of these couples were just like us having a real heartfelt desire to adopt a son or daughter, we met most of them at various training days that we attended, we kept in touch for many years, unfortunately not one of those couples to our knowledge adopted a child, some told us that they could not put up with all of the hassle and indifference they had received from social workers, others said that they could not put up any longer with the almost hostile and distrustful nature towards them by their social workers, some just quit before they were able to adopt a child.

Hollie and me are perhaps made of a bit stronger stuff, so keep that in mind all of you who really do want to adopt a child, please remember that it is sometimes sadly like a challenging battle, we have proved that this battle can be won.

There are lots of reasons why people want to adopt a child, in our case we always longed to have a child, you might have had children who have flown the nest and your home now feels quiet and empty, it may be that you just feel in your heart that you would like to help one of those dear children who is stuck in a children's care home, it could be that you have married later in life and feel that you would love to have a child to complete your family, there are scores of reasons why you might want to adopt a child, please remember that it may take a fair amount of time, so don't put off till tomorrow, what you can do today.

Stick To Your Goal

Might we encourage anyone reading this story who is trying to adopt a child or children, the secret is to stick to your goal, many of you embarking on this course may well find it to be a long and winding road, you may even find that you have to fight every inch of the way, it can be difficult, even so, always remember, keep going forward, keeping your eyes on the prize, success can quite often be much nearer than we think, so never give up, even if you feel like giving up, don't ever quit, a fight can be won if you persevere, at the end of your journey, a little child's future life, welfare and health could well be in your loving hands.

In the eyes of your local authority social services department with all of its red tape and the social workers they employ who the bulk of them in our experience view heterosexual married couples with disdain and suspicion, you may be too fat, too old, you might not even have the right colour skin, maybe you are too southern, too white middle class, you might not have the correct ethnic back round, you may even be a member of a fringe political party, from our experiences we can add a number of things too that list, you may have a shallow river on your property, even if you offer to spend a small fortune to fence it off on both sides, they may well consider it too dangerous and not let you adopt a child, they will however living under the same circumstances allow you to foster a child?

Very strange people these social workers it is quite possible that you live on a farm as we once did, once again in social workers eyes, that is thought to be extremely dangerous! Shock Horror! I can here them saying to each other; 'Do you know these people, who I met today actually want to adopt a child and give one of our children in care a loving family home and they 'Live on a Farm!' they will very likely have chickens, sheep, pigs, cows and

136

even horses on those farms you know and they create all of that smelly horse muck and heaven forbid a combine harvester and scourge upon scourge a tractor.'

Once again there was absolutely no hope whatsoever of us adopting a child when we lived on the farm, however we had a follow up letter from social services to tell us that we could attend a training course to foster a child at the same address on that very same farm. That's even stranger.
They always told us that the children come first and that the children are at the front of their minds? There is some hope of that. Weird People!!

You may even be told "That it is not every woman's God given right to have a child" and have those words spoken very harshly to you by a toffee nosed, very rude social worker, or you just might live in a trendy area, or indeed have a large house, the reason for all of these anomalies or aberrations, its because grossly inconsiderate social workers, pontificate, moralize and decide, Just Who Do They Think They Are?

Once again, you have NO! chance of adopting a child. You may even be in a social workers eyes not a perfect match?, Isn't it about time that local authority social workers who behave in such a childish manner, need to grow up and start acting their age and start living in the real world, and get on with the work of placing children with the people who care far more about the welfare of these vulnerable children than most of these social workers ever will.

I Wouldn't Mind A Quick Peek Inside His Home

These are just a small selection of the hurdles that you may have to jump over or the rings you might have too jump through in order to satisfy the whims and fancies of these often very domineering people.
It seems pretty obvious to me that these social workers definitely try and think of every implausible, dubious, ridiculous, inconceivable, far-fetched excuses to try to prevent ordinary every day nice people from adopting a child.
And if like us you might even be unlucky enough to come across an agency worker who thinks that your home is a' Bit too clean and tidy' for you to be considered worthy enough to adopt one of their children, I must admit I wouldn't mind having a quick peek inside his home.

We are promised new state rules coming into force with regard to the adoption system, hopefully all of the forgoing red tape, political

correctness will be swept aside, Don't Hold Your Breath,' even if it were to happen, the sad bit will be about all of this, the clock cannot be put back, all of the many thousands of children who were denied a forever loving home during all of this loopy period of madness, have missed out on a normal home life by either being stuck in a care home or fostered out to lots of different families with every hope of them ever finding a loving family to join; Gone!
All of those responsible need to be rooted out and severely dealt with.
I do not know how many of them sleep at night.

It is said that these social workers need to be retrained with new skills, there some hope of that for many of them! Remember that old saying 'A leopard cannot change its spots' they will in all likelihood, never change, just a few might, but the majority that we have met are so deeply entrenched in their impolite, discourteous, disrespectful domineering ways they, like the leopard can probably never change.
The decks need to be cleared now, new faces are urgently needed, people very carefully chosen, with strictly only those with a caring attitude, selected to do this vitally important job of helping these children.

There are lots of *small local voluntary adoption agencies* that may possibly help you to adopt a child, for instance try looking on-line.
If Hollie and myself made any mistakes, by far the worst one was approaching in the first instance a Local Authority Social Services Adoption Service, we will always regret that, they were the ones that we approached in the first instance and in my honest opinion they are not fit for purpose, although you will ultimately have to go through their awful Social Services adoption system in order to be able to adopt a child.

Our advice would be to let your chosen *small adoption agency* deal with them, it will save you an awful lot of unnecessary hassle, as they will have people with often vast experience of dealing with social services, whereas you will probably have little or no experience in dealing with these people and if they deal with you the same way as they dealt with Hollie and me, they will, Steam Roller over you and mess you around, because of your lack of experience.

Also its advisable to stick to a helpful one of the *smaller charity adoption agencies,* not the big money grabbing ones who pay their head people enormous amounts of money that could be put towards better use helping the children.

In the year 2010 only sixty babies were adopted nationwide, when at the time there were over three thousand five hundred babies in the care system.

Note also: that a white child is three times more likely to be adopted than a black child, and it now takes well over twenty months on average for any child to be adopted, meaning a three year old child will be approaching five years old before being adopted.

However, in some areas of the country the time taken can be very much more than this. If you carefully think about those figures they show that you stand a far better chance of adopting an older child than trying to adopt a baby.

Latest figures show that the number of children successfully being adopted has gone up, with the close on four thousand being placed with families in a year, that is good news, however as with all figures given out by the State as usual one has to take a closer look to see if they might have been massaged in some way in order to make them look better than they really are, for instance a large amount of the children included in these figures are children adopted by their step parents, and people going abroad to find a child to adopt a child. Nevertheless, there will hopefully be a much better future in store for the children who have been adopted, we should all rejoice over that, even so, take note that the total number in State care has *not gone down in number* as more and more children are joining that total every year, so as I understand it, the total number of children in care remains around the same as were in care at the start of the year, for the sake of those children these figures need urgently to reduce each year.

As there are so many older children in care, might I encourage you all to consider adopting an older child, in our case Lucy was seven years old when she first came to live with us, do not be put off by the thought of adopting an older child, these are the children who are usually bypassed when it comes to people choosing a child to adopt, please consider one of these dear children, they really do respond to love despite what any social worker might tell you, in our case, Lucy has brought both Hollie and myself a huge amount of joy and I can assure you one hundred per cent that our Lucy did respond to the love that we gave her.

These are the children who really need us to help them, teach them, help them to get over the often very traumatic experiences that they may well have suffered in the awful care system, where it seems that they are largely out of sight and out of mind.

Can you find a place in your heart to want to help one of these children, and if you can find one of these children, care for them and give them all of the love that your heart can possibly muster, in order to give them a decent life as part of your loving family, that is something that all children surely must deserve, if you do decide to do that, I stress don't ever give up, this whole adoption process can be very cruel and challenging, full of political correctness and a lot of totally unnecessary red tape dished out by overbearing social workers.

Why any government of any country especially a so-called wealthy country like ours, cannot put more effort into helping these children in care, I am truly amazed, they pour £Billions of pounds into war and other wasteful scatterbrain things, but it seems, cannot help a child in need.
I also reiterate that I find it very hard to understand just why the State sets such a high standard for prospective adopters, as most people who have their own children, if given the same tests would in all probability very likely fail miserably to adopt their own children.

Lucy is now nineteen years old and has grown up to be a fine young lady, she has a job that she absolutely loves, has passed her driving test and saved up to buy herself a car, in which she takes great pleasure in taking mum and dad out for a drive, why only last week she took us on a ninety mile round trip to a popular seaside resort and treated her mum and dad to lunch, we both felt proud of our daughter for the very fact of what she has achieved thus far in her life.

She has been a real blessing for us both and now we could not possibly imagine our lives without her, she is just like a breath of fresh air, young vibrant full of life, we both love her to bits, and she tells us every day and every night before going to bed that she loves us both "Love you mum, Love you dad" would we do it all again? You bet we would, our lives have been enriched beyond compare.

We have helped Lucy to transform her life for the better, but it never ever occurred to us that she would transformed our lives for the better, but she has, we have been blessed far beyond what any words could ever describe and all of this came about by a lovely little girl named Lucy.

A Very Big Thank You

Our deepest and warmest thanks go to all of those wonderful people who helped us to be able to adopt our Lucy, in no particular order because they

were all very special people, Jacob Jones, Thank You, Sandra Good, Thank You, Brenda Nice, Thank You, Felicity Cool, Thank You and not forgetting Molly Sinclair, Thank You, Hollie and myself are indebted to you all, we cannot possibly forget your having faith in us to look after our little Lucy, there is not one single day that goes past without you coming into our thoughts, you all helped to make our life complete.
Thank You all from the bottom of our hearts.

And a very special big Thank You to all of you people whoever you are, for joining us by reading this story about our experiences in life and in our quest to adopt a child, we sincerely hope that by reading our account of the way that things actually happened and finally worked out in our effort to adopt a child, you have been able to see just some of the trials, problems, worries and the pitfalls that can occur when trying to adopt a child, we have tried very hard to put into words what we experienced, its not all negative, thankfully, although there were far more problems than there should have been, mainly brought about by many callous often extremely rude box tickers who seemed to have a distinct lack of fellow feeling for these unfortunate children, there were also many treasured moments of elation and sheer joy and happiness brought about by many of our experiences.

Now we know and are both a little more aware of what is really going on when someone decides to adopt a child, I still find the whole business to be an absolutely confusing, disorganizational mess.
A loving family wants to adopt a child and an often neglected little child needs a forever mum and dad, its that simple really, and the powers that be make such a huge kerfuffle or a mountain out of a molehill about it all and who suffers, everybody concerned with the case and especially the young child who is getting older and will probably end up as being much harder to place with a family, meaning he or she will in all likelihood end up in a dreaded children's secret care home.

The answers? You Tell Me? I fully accept that there may always be a few hiccups along the way in placing these children very much more quickly, even so, what about for instance if there was a dedicated team of people assembled in each area of the country to sort out any problems almost immediately as they arise, like for instance the getting together of the wonderful bunch of individuals just mentioned who helped us, all of these people without exception had a heartfelt love for children, therefore, they would all sing from the same hymn sheet and mountains can then be

moved, as jointly the child's welfare would be their major concern.
Not all of this waiting for years, these children need a loving home like yesterday, delays can and do have severe repercussions on a child's health and future development.

Many of you perhaps may be finding it hard to believe what really goes on in the children's so called care system, there is certainly a lot of hurt and abuse, with many social workers and children's home carers just not giving the children in the horrible care system the heartfelt care that these children deserve. Its very sad, but unfortunately true, and just think that you! Yes you! Can do something about it, firstly never take No! for an answer, when it comes to adopting a child.

You may like us, even have to move house even to another area of the country, you may have to put up with difficult or rude social workers until you find the right one to help you, we have proved beyond any doubt that there are some people out there within social services who are like precious gems who brilliantly shine as they stood head and shoulders above those who just carry on in a very mundane way, these people I am talking about are different and are always ready to point you in the right direction, like gems they are hard to find, but they are out there and are ready willing and able to help you to adopt a child.

Every one of you dear people, please stay strong, do not ever despair, face life with hope, determination and courage, face up to the upsets and do not ever give up, remember we can all succeed if we are prepared to go the extra mile.
We genuinely hope that you have enjoyed a very small glimpse into the world of adoption as Hollie and Myself have experienced it over the last twenty three years, if you are planning to adopt a child, may Hollie, Lucy and myself, wish you every lasting success.

Please always remember, don't ever give up, as the future life of some dear little person may well be in your loving hands

Bless You All   Hollie, Jenson and Lucy Speed